HOW TO READ THE

AURA

AND PRACTICE
PSYCHOMETRY,
TELEPATHY, &
CLAIRVOYANCE

HOW TO READ THE

AURA

AND PRACTICE
PSYCHOMETRY,
TELEPATHY, &
CLAIRVOYANCE

W. E. BUTLER

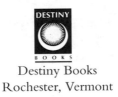

Destiny Books
Rochester, Vermont

Destiny Books
One Park Street
Rochester, Vermont 05767
www.InnerTraditions.com

Destiny Books is a division of Inner Traditions International

LIBRARY OF CONGRESS CATALOGING-IN-PUBLICATION DATA

Butler, W. E. (Walter Ernest), 1898-
    How to read the aura, practice psychometry, telepathy, and clairvoyance.
    "Bring together, under one cover, four companion works by . . . W. E.
Butler"—Foreword.
    1. Psychical research.   I. Title.
BF1031.B895   1987   133.8   87-13450
ISBN 0-89281-161-7
ISBN 0-89281-705-4

Printed and bound in the United States

10 9 8 7

Contents

Foreword

DESTINY Books is particularly pleased to bring together under one cover, four companion works by the distinguished British parapsychologist, W.E. Butler. These practical manuals for the development of the four basic parapsychological faculties have enjoyed great popular appreciation in England and many prominent psychics owe their introduction in the field to the Butler technique.

Parapsychology or psychic research is a subject of interest to an ever-increasing number of people. The extraordinarily well-publicized phenomena produced by Uri Geller, the far-reaching and beneficial work of Edgar Cayce earlier in this century, and most recently the groundbreaking discovery of aura photography by Semyon and Valentina Kirlian, have brought to public awareness the existence of psychic capacities beyond the frontier of the ordinary.

The reality of these capacities is no longer in question save by dyed-in-the-wool skeptics. They do exist and what's more, experts in the field such as Butler, tell us that these faculties are latent in us all and are not the exclusive possession of a few "freaks of nature" or "genetic mutants." Clairvoyance, telepathy, psychometry and aura-vision are skills which must be cultivated and exercised in order to develop. Butler has outlined the simplest possible methods, requiring a minimum of apparatus, by which any interested reader can instruct himself in the art of extrasensory perception.

Intuition is the keystone of all the parapsychological faculties. Current research on the human brain states that, on the average, man employs only about ten percent of his total mental capacity. As the science of parapsychology advances and neurologists observe the brain processes of psychics, it may be found that other areas of the brain are utilized to receive and transmit knowledge about the world via a non-sensory mode.

Our normal way of knowing is through the senses. We know that the sapphire before us is blue, because we receive that information via the sensory apparatus of the eyes. When a psychic knows that the object in the next room, or thousands of miles away, is a blue gemstone, or a sapphire, she or he knows it through a faculty of the mind that transcends the senses. Extrasensory perception has its roots in intuition.

Everybody has and uses intuition to some degree, although its function varies widely from individual to individual. But anyone who has experienced the almost supernatural relief of following through a strong hunch and finding it to have been accurate, will recognize the value that a more developed, consciously controlled utilization of intuition could offer. The problem with intuition as it's found in modern man is its unreliability. It's not always present when needed, and when present, it may be so faint and unaccustomed, that we hesitate to act on it.

It has been observed that humanity, living in tribal conditions, uses and relies on intuitive faculty to a much greater extent than the average man in the so-called civilized nations. Our intuitive capacity has been lost in direct proportion to the development of reason and empiricism.

The methods for developing the higher faculties of the mind have been known to humanity all over the world. But they have always been a carefully guarded secret, revealed only to aspirants (usually in initiation ceremonies), after they had demonstrated their worthiness, maturity, responsibility and ethical preparedness. There was good reason for such secrecy and exclusiveness! Intuition, evolved to the point of true parapsychological capacity, confers enormous power on an individual and such power in the wrong hands can wreak havoc and destruction. The most preeminent example of this is the case of Hitler and the Nazi party. The Nazis wanted to restore to the "Aryan race" the magical or parapsychological powers that they believed it had possessed, prior to the conversion of the Germanic tribes to Christianity. In the special training schools for the SS elite and through genetic selection, they hoped to develop a type of *superman*, which collectively would form a "master race" to dominate the rest of the world. They programmatically attempted to replace reason with "magical" intuition, compassion with cruelty and ethical responsibility with brute strength.

If rightly undertaken, the rediscovery and systematic development of the parapsychological intuition could undoubtedly greatly benefit humanity. But the foregoing example demonstrates that the process is fraught with danger. Man is part of a cosmic evolutionary process; therefore any attempt to regress to a prior, primitive condition is unnatural and devolutionary. The evolutionary path points in the direction of a recovery and integration of intuition with reason and responsibility, which have taken so many centuries to evolve.

Esotericists seem to agree that a major characteristic of the Aquarian Age, which we are moving into, is the unveiling of esoteric knowledge, hitherto secret. The Age of Aquarius is to be an aeon of individual responsibility and personal quest for enlightened, spiritual evolution. Therefore it is up to each individual who acquires this book and decides to take up the exciting course of study and development which it offers, to look to the purity and selflessness of his own motives. For "As ye sow, so shall ye reap." Whatever selfishness or harmfulness is committed through the normal or paranormal faculties of mind will inevitably redound against the committer, and conversely, selfless and beneficial actions will advance the doer and increase his power to serve his fellow men.

The benefits from the expansion of our awareness

beyond the borders of the senses, through to intuition, are truly innumerable. Take for example the development of aura-vision. How much deeper our understanding and how much more effectively might we relate to others if we could actually perceive the moods and mental states they labored under by seeing the changing colors of their aura! How much easier to avoid being drawn into others' negative states of mind, if we could perceive with certainty the mechanistic aspect of what's occurring. Esotericists with developed aura-vision have long claimed that conditions of disease usually manifest visibly in the aura's energy field before appearing on the physical plane. By being alert to this, we might be of enormous assistance to ourselves and others, by warning them in advance of imminent danger to their health.

Psychometry is the utilization of intuition to "read" the history or biography of physical objects. What makes this possible, according to traditional esoteric theory, is that matter receives into its structure the strong mental, spiritual and emotional impressions that occur in relation to it. An object of major historical significance, such as the British crown, would be positively resonant with impressions accumulated over the centuries of strife and change. A psychometrist could read deeply into an aspect of history that is rarely covered by the history books by tuning into the emanations from such an object. Thus, it is easy to see how psychometry could be of great use and value to historians, antique lovers, museum aficionados, anthropologists and archaeologists, to name only the obvious.

In spite of the innumerable examples of authenticated parapsychological phenomena, the scientific establishment is still reluctant to officially recognize their existence. Established worldviews are deeply entrenched and the evidence for paranormal mental powers cuts deeply into the prevalent scientific materialism. Despite this, governmental intelligence agencies in both Russia and America are not standing on ceremony for scientific sanction. Wherever advantage in the balance of power is to be obtained, both the KGB and the CIA are making headway in the exploitation of these powers for espionage and intelligence gathering. In August 1977, Admiral Stansfield Turner, then head of the CIA, was reported by the press as admitting that the CIA had exploited an individual's developed clairvoyance for spying at a distance on our enemies. The exploitation of his faculty had continued up until his death. In July 1977, the papers were full of the story of an American reporter who was detained in the U.S.S.R. for attempting to smuggle out documents pertaining to top secret Russian research in the field of parapsychology. The 1984-ish implications of such research, presently in progress, should give every thoughtful person reason for concern.

The existence of paranormal powers is no longer a matter of speculation or hearsay. With the Butler techniques, you can now have evidence of their actuality through personal experience. Parapsychological development can enrich your own life and that of others by opening new, deeply satisfying dimensions that offer opportunity for a lifetime of exploration and research.

PART I

Clairvoyance

1

What Is Clairvoyance?

WE think it was Dr. Johnson, the famous wit and philosopher immortalized by his friend Boswell, who once said, "Define your terms, gentlemen, define your terms. It saves argument!" This advice is very helpful when we are dealing with a subject such as "Clairvoyance." The name has gathered to itself so many meanings that before you can really begin to get to work on the development of the clairvoyant faculty, you should know something of the nature of that which you are trying to unfold. To do otherwise is to risk getting mixed up in all kinds of complications. So the first step is to get a general idea of the nature of this wonderful power.

The word "clairvoyance" with its associated words "clairaudience" and "clairsentience" comes from the French, and these were used by the followers of Dr. Franz Anton Mesmer, who popularized the practice of what was then known as "Animal Magnetism," later to be called after him "Mesmerism." A certain amount of mesmeric work was later rechristened by Dr. James Braid. He called it "Hypnotism" and under his name that particular fragment of the mesmeric technique has become respectable; there is even a Medical Society of Hypnotists! Drs. Esdaile and Elliotson, together with many others of their profession who were bitterly persecuted by the medical orthodoxy of their day, must surely have smiled, a little ruefully perhaps, when in the after-life they were told of the formation of a Society of *Medical* Hypnotists.

The popular idea of mesmerism, by the way, is a good deal removed from the actual truth, though we suspect that it will be with us for many a long day. It largely stems from the image of the sinister mesmerist Svengali, in du Maurier's *Trilby*, a book which was a best-seller of its time.

In the course of their researches, the early mesmerists discovered that some of their patients, when in deep mesmeric trance, showed signs of what today is known as ESP—"Extrasensory Perception." They didn't have this very convenient term so they used other names, such as those we have already given. However, in modern times new names have been given, many of them derived from Greek and Latin words. This is because there was, and still is, a great deal of superstition, silliness and fraud associated with the old names, and it was felt necessary to break away from the old associations. In this respect, the poet was possibly right when he asked "What's in a name?" The flower of supernormal vision is just as real a thing when it is called "metagnomy" or ESP, as when it is known as "clairvoyance."

The three words "clairvoyance," "clairaudience" and "clairsentience" mean "clear vision," "clear hearing" and "clear sensing" respectively, and, of course, they do not refer to the ordinary physical senses but rather to supernormal or superphysical sense perceptions. Since, however, these superphysical perceptions do not enter our minds through our physical senses, where, then, do they have their origin? The short answer, and one which we believe to be correct, is that they come from the subconscious levels of our mind. Modern psychology has shown that certain levels of the mind exist behind or below the ordinary waking consciousness, and it is in these levels that clairvoyance has its point of emergence. For the purpose of this book and to simplify the issue we may say that we all possess a finer body of superphysical substance, and that the "senses" of that finer body can be connected to the waking consciousness so that what we perceive in those finer levels of substance may be *consciously* perceived, for it is fairly certain that even though we may not *consciously* receive these superphysical sense reports, they are being constantly received in the deeper mind both when we are awake and when we sleep.

In the East there has been worked out an elaborate scheme of psychic development which refers to an intricate set of links, known as "the *Chakras*," which can be developed in order that superphysical perceptions may be brought *through the subconscious* into the waking mind. You will notice that we emphasize the fact that they are brought *through* the subconscious, and this is true of course of the real supernormal powers. There are, however, many cases of visions, voices and other sense-perceptions where it is fairly easy for the psychologist to prove that they originate *in* the subconscious and are, in fact, due to certain stresses and strains therein. There is a great difference between the ESP images and those born in the subconscious, but in both cases the images, sounds, and so on are built up in accordance with the laws governing the workings of that subconscious level. It is important that you realize that although your visions may be genuine ESP, they are likely to become somewhat distorted as they pass through to your waking self. This distorting action is well known to all who have had practical experience of these matters. The late W. T. Stead, a veteran journalist and social reformer, called this "the stained glass effect," and this gives a very good picture of the action of the subconscious. Just as a stained-glass window imposes its own patterns and colors upon the white light which streams through it, so does the subconscious stain and distort all that passes through it to the waking self.

As a matter of fact, even when we are using our ordinary physical senses the same distorting action takes place, though to a lesser degree. We see that which our subconscious "keys" us to see, and often entirely miss things which are seen by others who are looking at the same scene. This is well known to police and lawyers, who have to deal with eye-witness accounts of accidents and other occurrences. It is asserted by occultists that the incoming clairvoyant or other psychic impressions may make use of two different nerve systems in our body. They may come by way of what is known as the "involuntary nervous system" or by way of the "cerebro-spinal system." If they come via the involuntary nervous system, the "Gates of Ivory" as they were known in ancient times, they may be vague and difficult to define. The images themselves may be clear, but the meanings which they are intended to deliver to the waking self are not clearly perceived. Also, in very many cases, this form of vision is not under the control of the will of the person concerned. Often when it is needed it cannot be brought into action, and at other times, when it is not required, it breaks through into the waking consciousness. You will easily see that this could be dangerous under certain circumstances. The other mode of working, through the voluntary nervous system, has the advantage of being under the control of the psychic, and can be aroused at will. It is also far less dependent upon what, in psychic experimentation, are known as "conditions."

However, having said all this, we must also add that the use of one form of psychism alone is very rare, despite what some "authorities" may say. Over fifty years of practical experience in this field has taught us that it is very seldom that the so-called "positive psychic" is using entirely the voluntary nerve system. He may achieve ninety-nine percent of such control on good days, but on others he may be only fifty-five percent "positive." In the same way the psychic using the involuntary nervous system may, on very good days, begin to work through the voluntary nerves. In fact, both "positive" and "negative" psychics work on a kind of "sliding scale," for the two nerve systems are closely linked together. Although the voluntary system should be the dominant partner, all the processes by which the senses, whether they be physical or superphysical, communicate their messages to the waking self are processes that are carried out by the involuntary nervous system working through the machinery of the subconscious mind.

We have said this because we wish to blur the distinction that has been established by many theoretical occultists between the two forms of psychic activity. At the same time we want to emphasize that you *must* establish some measure of control over your psychic activity right from the moment you begin your training. Of course, during the early stages of that training you have to give the developing faculty a considerable amount of leeway, but, gently and persistently, voluntary control must be imposed on it.

It is quite possible, bearing in mind the current attitude to the subject, that your ideas as to what clairvoyance really is are somewhat mixed. The name is applied to many things, and this often leads to considerable confusion. So we will try to describe in as simple a way as possible what clairvoyance is. First of all, however, we want to deal with a form of clairvoyance which is in reality an extension of the ordinary physical sight. If you take a prism, which is a three-sided glass bar, and pass a beam of white light through it, the white light is split up into a band of colors ranging from red at the one end to violet at the other. We know also that below the color vibration "red" there are "infra-red" rays, and above or beyond the violet end of this colored spectrum are other rays, including the "ultra-violet" rays, the X-rays and many others. In fact our visible band of colors is only a section of a very great range of vibration.

Now if, having thrown your colored band of light onto a white background, you invite half a dozen people to mark just where, on the white card, the limits of the color band seem to them to be situated, you will find that the results will vary in sometimes a spectacular way. You may find that one person places the limits well *within* the red end, and well *beyond* the violet end. Others will apparently see more beyond the red end and see even less of the violet end, but most of the people with whom you do this experiment will see the band of color in the same general way. This particular variation depends upon the structure of the retina, the screen in the eye upon which the lens of the eye projects a picture of whatever you may be looking at. There are, of course, other factors, but these

19

are not recognized by the orthodox medical faculty, as they belong to the superphysical levels.

This experiment shows that some people are able to perceive light vibrations which are invisible to others, and this is why we have referred to it. Through the years a very considerable amount of experimental proof has been obtained in support of the teachings of the followers of Mesmer, and others too, that the physical body has a counterpart of much finer matter, and that this finer body is the mold upon which the physical body is built up. This finer body also has its senses, and these are capable of perceiving the various conditions of the world of finer matter of which this "etheric body" is built up.

The use of the name "etheric" arouses a good deal of contempt from the physicists, who regard the word "ether" as one of their own particular possessions.

It is taught that through the etheric double the vital forces enter the physical body, and that the mind and emotions are able to be expressed through all the cells, glands and nerves of the body. It is also taught that the senses of this finer body can also be linked up with the waking consciousness, and there are certain methods of doing this. We will discuss this matter of the development of etheric vision and audition when we come to deal with the actual work of psychic training.

The etheric vision is sometimes called "X-ray vision" as it allows its possessor to see through physical matter. In the early days of mesmerism it was developed for the medical diagnosis of diseases, and since the etheric clairvoyant can, in some cases, apparently see into the interior of the human body and closely observe the working of its various organs, it is easy to see how very helpful this form of clairvoyance can be.

There are certain devices which, it is claimed, enable this form of vision to be developed. Special dyes, such as the coal-tar dye dycyanine, are dissolved in alcohol, and the liquid poured into a cell formed by cementing together two pieces of plain glass, leaving a small gap between them. The experimenter looks at a source of light through this colored screen for a certain time and then, after some perseverance in the technique, he may begin to see the emanations which are constantly being given off by all living things. The theory is that the practice alters the retina or screen of the eye (the "rods" and "cones" as the minute nerve endings which make up that screen are called) thus enabling the eye to respond to rays of light which are beyond the visible color spectrum. There are also spectacles, "auraspecs," with colored glass inserts, which, it is claimed, produce the same effect as the dycyanine screens.

The pioneer work on this line of research was done by a medical electrician, W. J. Kilner at St. Thomas's Hospital in London, a good many years ago. He published an account of his work in a book entitled *The Human Aura*. I will treat etheric sight in the last section of this book, covering the aura and its phenomena.

Having dealt in a general way with this etheric clairvoyance, we will go on to other types, and here we may divide our subject into four fairly definite varieties of working. We have therefore

(a) Psychological Clairvoyance.
(b) Spatial Clairvoyance.
(c) Astral Clairvoyance.
(d) True Spiritual Clairvoyance.

In the next chapter, we will consider these four aspects of our subject, and then, having given you a fair foundation, we will proceed to the actual work of development.

2

Types of Clairvoyance

IN the last chapter, we listed four varieties of clairvoyant experience. We shall deal with them separately, though in actual practice it is always difficult to do this, since the faculty that we are using along any one level, although directed by us, may well suddenly bring in new levels of perception when we do not desire their manifestation. However, for convenience of study we will differentiate between these forms of the faculty and deal with them separately.

Psychological Clairvoyance

This is a name we have invented ourselves to cover a certain type of clairvoyance, and we think that when you have read what we have to say about it, you will be able to see why we chose it. Most of us are familiar with those curious attractions and repulsions which we feel for many people. "I do not like thee, Dr. Fell" runs the old verse, and it goes on to say "The reason why, I cannot tell." There are some people whom we instinctively and spontaneously like or dislike, and very often "the reason why" we cannot tell, is that the feeling comes to us from the depths of our subconscious. However, *it need not* necessarily be due to clairvoyant perception; there is a perfectly sound psychological explanation of this sympathy or antipathy. It may be as well if we get this purely psychological point out of the way before we go any further.

In most of our lives there have been some people who, in one way or another, have caused us to experience pain or shame or fear on the one hand, and joy, happiness and confidence on the other. We have forgotten the people and the incidents with which they were connected, and for many years we may never have even thought of them at all. However, the memories have not been lost; they have simply been pushed out of sight into the depths of the subconscious. It is very important, if we would maintain true psychological balance and self-control, that such memories should not be pushed too deeply into the depths, as under these circumstances they may become a kind of mental and emotional cancer, blocking the free flow of vitality and interfering with the orderly working of the mind.

However, such memories are very often forgotten. Then one day we meet someone whose face or bearing strongly resembles that of our former friend or enemy, and although we do not consciously remember that person, the newly met person strikes a chord in our memory. Although the *mental* recollection of the friend or enemy of old does not arise, something else does, and that is the *emotional affect*, the feelings which used to be aroused, and this emotional charge is "projected" upon the stranger we have met. So we "feel" that "Dr. Fell," who may quite possibly be a good and likable man, is someone we must distrust and fear. This psychological projection is quite common; and it does explain many of the sudden "likings" and "dislikings" which affect us.

In many other cases, however, subsequent events prove that our instinct was perfectly correct. Here we come to a point which is often overlooked when clairvoyance is being discussed. We are liable to think of clairvoyance as simple vision, but it is quite different. This psychic faculty, as it rises through the subconscious, brings much more with it than a simple visual picture; there is also a combined mental and emotional atmosphere or "affect" that surrounds it. It is the sum of visual image, emotional feeling and mental ideas which come into the waking consciousness when we exercise the clairvoyant faculty. We shall see this again when we come to consider the part played by "symbols" in clairvoyance.

At the beginning of development, this mixed emotional-mental atmosphere is usually more vivid than any simple visual image, but, as it proceeds, the image becomes more definite and the atmosphere less prominent. Following this, the visual images seem to give way to some extent to a curious formless intuitional understanding, and this may well become an entirely formless perception, in which all the details that the visual images and the mental-emotional atmosphere gave are superseded by a clear and exceedingly definite perception. Without picture or atmosphere this gives to the waking self a full, definite and comprehensive understanding of whatever is being observed.

We do not say that this will be the automatic sequence of development. You will find the first stage to be the one which seems best for you. Others may find that they seem to start on the second level, where image and intuition work together, and others again may find themselves starting on the third level of perception. We may illustrate this point by an imaginary example of the workings of these three phases. Suppose we are called into a so-called haunted house, and we take with us three clairvoyants, each working on a different level of perception. Let us see what our clairvoyant of the first level would probably experience. Sitting in the haunted room, he might see faint patches of phosphorescence in various parts, faintly luminous clouds wreathing around him, and he would "feel" very strongly certain emotional currents in the room. These would cause similar emotions to arise in his mind, emotions of depression and gloom. As the power intensified, he might see the faintly luminous figure of an elderly man sitting in the chair opposite, staring moodily at the fireplace. (This description is based upon an actual experience which we had some years ago, when we were called upon to "exorcise" the ghost who haunted this room.) With our clairvoyant of the first type, the "atmosphere" would be far more definite than the image of the man, and he would be liable to react to this atmosphere in a marked way.

Our clairvoyant of the second type would not be affected so strongly by the atmosphere of depression and gloom, but he would be able to observe the visual image of the man more closely and calmly, and he would quite possibly become aware that what he was looking at was not the real man, but an imprint or "shade" of someone who had lived in that house and used that room. There is a subtle but real difference between these imprints on the psychic atmosphere and the presence of a living being. It is difficult to describe the difference; gradually one becomes aware of the "quality" of the life within the form which is perceived. In this case our clairvoyant would find a curious unreal feeling with this form, whereas if he were looking at a living being he would feel the personal power and individuality of the man. We shall return to this point when we consider the question of symbols and their use in clairvoyance.

Our third type of clairvoyant would, as it were, "run up the scale." Opening up his clairvoyant faculty, he would first become aware of the strongly charged psychic atmosphere of the room, and then, stepping up his perception, he would see, clearly and distinctly, the form which his two friends had also seen. Like the second seer, he would know that the form was simply "an image in the astral light," as he might describe it. Now, stepping up his vision, he would for a moment or two lose both "form" and "atmosphere," and into his mind would rise a "block of knowledge," if we may so describe it. He would know, without a shadow of doubt, how the atmosphere of gloom, depression and suicide had been built up in that room; he would know also how it had been maintained in such power since its first creation, and he would be aware of what steps must be taken to destroy it and cleanse the place that it might once again be habitable.

In this particular case, the clairvoyant diagnosis and later treatment which we were able to give proved effective, and on making enquiries, we found that our clairvoyant findings were correct. We found that some ten years before our visit, the tenant at that time was a rather dull-witted farm laborer. For many years before his death by suicide he had been in the habit of returning from his work, sitting in this room and brooding over his real and imaginary wrongs. Finally he had committed suicide. The atmosphere he had left behind him was pretty deadly, as we can vouch from our own experience; we felt the strong suicidal impulse ourselves, and it was a common experience of anyone who sat in that room for any length of time.

This was an actual experience, but if you wish to read a fictional representation by a master of the storyteller's art, we can recommend you read Rudyard Kipling's short story entitled "The House Surgeon." There is a poem which goes with it, called "The Rabbi's Song," and one verse of this may be of interest:

If thought can reach to Heaven, on Heaven let it dwell,
For fear like power is given to thought, to reach to Hell;
For fear the desolation and darkness of thy mind
Perplex and vex a dwelling which thou has left behind.

Of course, there are powerful and beneficent forces and influences that radiate from the very stones of those places which, through the centuries, have been true houses of prayer and praise, and where the two worlds have drawn closely together through the work of faithful pastors and loving people. These atmospheres may be perceived by the clairvoyant, and you will learn by direct experience that you, too, have a grave responsibility for those conditions which you are continually forming around you for the help or hindrance of your fellow man. For it is indeed true, as the Bible says: "No man liveth to himself alone."

We trust that this illustration of clairvoyant practice will enable you to see what we have been driving at in these last few pages. Clairvoyance is not quite so simple as some would make it out to be, but these three levels are those generally encountered. Clairvoyance along these lines is also of great assistance in what we may term "psychic counseling" and clairvoyants of all three types can do good work therein. If we have made it seem that the third type is the best of the three, it is not because we wish you to regard the other two as being inferior. They are inferior in one sense, since they are stages in the development of the third type, and this we regard as the highest aspect of this level of psychic perception. There are higher levels, but these we shall deal with when we come to the form of clairvoyance which we have termed Spiritual Clairvoyance.

Clairvoyance in Space and Time

We now come to what we have named "Spatial Clairvoyance": that is, clairvoyance in space and time. Here we find two different methods used by clairvoyants of this kind. To explain this, we must go back to the time of the American Civil War. General Polk found that whenever he touched a piece of brass, even in pitch darkness, he experienced a curious metallic taste. This isolated fact interested a Dr. Rhodes Buchanan, who experimented with his students by getting them to hold vials containing powerful drugs. He found that some of the students, almost immediately after holding such vials, began to show the symptoms which would have been produced in them by an actual dose of the drug in question. His researches, in turn, attracted the attention of Professor Denton, a noted geologist of his time, who experimented with the aid of his sister, Mrs. Ann Denton Cridge.

He found that if she held a geological specimen to her forehead, she was able to see, in visual images, something of its past history. He carried out an exhaustive series of tests, in which he cut out any possibility of telepathic action between himself and his sister. The results of his researches were published in a book entitled *The Soul of Things*. This power of reading the past through the use of some object as a center of concentration he named "psychometry."

In its simplest terms, psychometry is really clairvoyance in time, using an object as a starting point and point of reference. Actually, it can be exercised without using an object, but concentration upon it helps to keep the clairvoyant faculty working within certain chosen limits. As we say, the object can be omitted and many people exercise this clairvoyance in time without having any idea of what they are doing. Some find that, although they are not aware of possessing any psychic power, when they are touching old furniture or antiques, dim pictures and emotions arise in their minds. This dim clairvoyant perception is far more common than is generally realized.

It is fairly easy for us to think of a cosmic picture gallery, a kind of living cinematographic record of everything that has happened in the world. It has been called the *Anima Mundi*: the "Soul of the World," and in the East, the Akashic Record. In ancient Egypt the record which was read out when the soul of a dead person was judged in the after-life was understood to be this imperishable record, and in the Christian Bible, in the Revelations of St. John, it is said that the books were opened, and the souls were judged by their record. It is possible that this image of the Book of Records was in the mind of the seer who wrote the book of Revelations, but it may also be that in both religions there was a knowledge of the existence of this cosmic record.

Now we come to a very different and difficult aspect of the subject. We can understand the record of all that has happened being preserved as we have described, but how about those things which have not yet happened, but which are sometimes perceived by the clairvoyant? That such prevision is possible is established beyond any doubt. This aspect of clairvoyance in time is one of its greatest attractions, and through all recorded history this power of prevision has been sought after in all cultures and by many means. Some of the ways of bringing the faculty into action have been good, others have been most decidedly evil. For the developing clairvoyant this power of prevision is a very great attraction and a very great danger. It seems so wonderful to be able to foretell the future, that the young psychic is swept off his feet by a feeling of importance as he is consulted by those who wish to know what is going to happen to them in the future. Herein lies the danger, and it is a two-fold one. First of all, the feeling of importance may grow to such an extent as to make him an egomaniac, and secondly, he will tend to overwork his faculty and then find that it is no longer reliable.

How the faculty works we do not yet really understand, though there are many theories. However, there is one form of prevision that can bear a rational explanation. If we think of a man who is standing at the window of a tall building, looking down upon a busy street, we may picture him watching a lady who is doing a little window-shopping on the opposite side of the road. As his eyes range along the street he may also see a painter on top of a tall ladder and, just before the lady reaches the foot of that ladder, he may see the painter drop his paint can, which begins to fall toward the pavement. Estimating the speed at which the paint is falling, and the speed at which the lady is approaching the spot where the paint can will hit the pavement, our observer would be fully justified if he called out to the lady "You are going to have an accident in a moment!" If she continues at her present speed, and does not turn to look at some window display that catches her eye, and if the pot of paint continues to fall without hitting any projection on the building, the prophecy of our observer may well come true. But if the other factors we have mentioned do come into the picture, then the prophecy will fail or, if the paint splashes over a considerable area, the lady may have her dress spotted with paint from the burst tin, and therefore may be said to have had a slight accident.

This is a possible explanation of some prevision, though not of all. The clairvoyant observer sees the possible working out of certain forces connected with the person concerned, and as long as those forces continue as they are, the result may be calculated in the deeper mind of the clairvoyant. In other cases, however, this explanation is not possible, and we attempt to understand the paradox that a future effect may come before its cause. This, of course, seems to violate all the laws of mind, but in the realm of physics there are one or two significant things which seem to point to this possibility; for instance the observed fact than an electron, under certain conditions, can apparently be at two places at once!

This whole subject is bound up with the philosophic ideas of fate and free will, of the sequence of action and reaction, and is the happy hunting ground of all kinds of theorists, cranks and pseudo-philosophers. Let us be pragmatic and simply say, "Prevision is a fact. How it works we do not know, at present!"

In any case, it will be the practice of foretelling the future, rather than the theories about it, which will concern you when you have begun to develop your clairvoyant powers and have been unwise enough to tell your friends about it. Those who don't regard you as a case for psychiatric treatment may cause you a lot of trouble by their naive belief in the accuracy of your clairvoyance. To the general public the word clairvoyance means one or both of two things: you can either see "spirits" or you can foretell the future; or do both. However, the "discerning of spirits" is not so easy as the uninstructed think, and the foretelling of the future has its own pitfalls. There are very few clairvoyants who can steadily and consistently exercise the power of prevision, for you must bear in mind that the very fact that you are clairvoyant does not guarantee you prevision. All depends upon the kind of clairvoyant faculty you may develop.

However, you will be besieged by those who want their fortunes told and, if your clairvoyance does give you prevision, you must decide whether it is right for you to employ it for this purpose. This is not an easy matter; so much depends upon the conditions of your life. As a general rule, however, such a use of the power should be very sparingly exercised.

There are certain devices, such as the use of tea leaves or coffee grounds left in a cup, which can be used by the clairvoyant to direct his vision to the future as well as the Tarot Cards, Sand Geomancy* and the I'Ching which

---

* For more on Geomancy, see *The Oracle of Geomancy*, by Stephen Skinner, Warner/Destiny Books, 1977

may be used to awaken the clairvoyant faculty and direct it along this line of prevision. The power of all these methods lies in the operator himself, not in the tea leaves, coffee grounds, Tarot pictures, Geomantic dots in the sand or the positions taken by the falling sticks of the I'Ching.

There is a very real test that you must face. In this foretelling of the future, you are entering into a close relationship with the inner lives of those who consult you, with their hopes and fears and doubts. Your slightest word will be taken by many to be the voice of truth, and they will try to order their lives by your foretelling. Have you the moral right to put yourself in the position of the oracle? Your findings will be powerful suggestions acting on the minds of your sitters. Will you be able to bear the responsibility that you have accepted? Should one of your clients misunderstand your message, and thinking it means that disaster awaits her, commit suicide, will you be able to justify yourself at the bar of your conscience? These and many other issues are bound up in this question of fortune-telling, and you will need to think the matter over very seriously before coming to any decision.

Indeed, in all clairvoyant work you will begin to realize that you must be most careful in what you describe, and especially in the inferences that you draw from what you see.

Astral Clairvoyance

The next type of clairvoyance we have called "Astral Clairvoyance." By this we mean the perception of apparently living beings who have no physical body.

The Devas or "Shining Ones," the "Lordly Ones" of Celtic tradition, the naiads, the dryads and the oreads of Grecian belief, and the fairy-folk, the Spirits of the Elements; all these live and have their being in the etheric and astral realms. You may see some of these entities as your clairvoyance begins to unfold, and their activities form a fascinating field of study for the clairvoyant investigator.

It is in this field of clairvoyant work that you will need to exercise the greatest care, for you will be making conscious contact with living beings of many different kinds, and not all of them will be friendly. You will also have to cultivate the power to resist the "glamor" which some of these beings can exert over you.

The matter of that realm of existence which we have termed the "astral levels" is very different from that of the physical world, and this can cause considerable confusion in your first clairvoyant adventures in these realms. Here on earth, matter is stable and if we wish to build something, a house for example, we have to move various bits of matter from one place to another: bricks, tiles, beams, cement, and so on. Whether we employ mechanical help or use our own physical energy, we are always working against what we call the weight and inertia of physical matter.

On the astral levels, however, things are very different for the substance of that world is not so dense and inert, but plastic and capable of being molded by the power of thought and desire. So the astral scenery you will begin to see if your clairvoyance develops along this line is built up by the thoughts and emotions of those who dwell in it.

There are beings existing only on these astral and etheric levels and they create their own scenery and conditions, which are unintelligible to the human mind until it has been trained to perceive such non-human effects.

Because of the plastic nature of the astral, it is difficult for the clairvoyant who is just beginning to open up his psychic vision to find his way around; he is bewildered by the complexity of the world into which he is gazing. Because of this, and because of his own earth-conditioned consciousness, he will without a doubt make many mistakes before he can correctly understand that which he perceives in psychic vision.

The non-human intelligences of this astral level do not possess any form similar to that of man, but they do have their own forms. If the human clairvoyant does come into contact with such non-human beings, his subconscious gives them a "local habitation and a name." This usually is embodied in a traditional image. Thus, the four elements were visualized in medieval times as Gnomes, Sylphs, Undines and Salamanders. In other nations and at other times, they were given different forms by man, and Shakespeare in *Midsummer Night's Dream* has caused innumerable "fairy-forms" to be formed by the imaginations of countless theater goers. Such forms are quickly seized and made use of by the elemental spirits, and they are often seen by clairvoyants in such guises.

This great world of the astral is well named the World of Illusion. At the same time, the illusions are in the artifically created appearances of that world; in itself it is as real as any other realm of nature. We have given this brief outline of the astral conditions so that you may realize something of the amazing complexity of the subject, but for the purpose of this book it is not necessary to go into any further detailed consideration of the astral levels. Unless you undertake very special psychic investigation such detail is not really necessary—though, of course, the more you do know, the better are you able to use your gift. But just as in earthly life you gradually developed your powers and learned by experience to use them, so in this psychic realm experience is a good teacher.

Spiritual Clairvoyance

We come now to the last type of clairvoyance—that which we have termed "Spiritual Clairvoyance." Before we start to deal with this type of vision, we will consider the word "spiritual," as it is very often entirely misunderstood. There are certain schools of thought which, so we believe, have built a very unsound body of teachings upon such misunderstandings. We say we believe this to be so, but in these matters we can only put forward what we believe to be the truth, and since the approaches to truth vary enormously, we can only speak for ourselves, or for our particular school of thought.

We want you to consider with an open mind the ideas we are now going to put before you. The general idea of "spirit," where the idea of its reality is accepted, is of a state of being totally opposed to, and distinct from "matter," more especially the matter of the material world, and of the material body we use in that world. This idea of the total and complete opposition of "spirit" and "matter" is a teaching which crept into Christianity in its early days, and it is still with us. At one time it was active in the early Church as what is known as the "Manichean heresy." If matter is so absolutely evil and eternally opposed to spirit, then the best thing the religious person can do is to turn his back upon it, and concentrate entirely upon the virtues of the spirit. More particularly should be repudiate and deny all the natural instincts of the physical body he is wearing, this "vile" body, as he would regard it. However, there have always been those, inside Christianity as well as outside it, who have repudiated this narrow and perverted view of life. In our own day, we see just such a repudiation of the Puritan outlook, however, some are carrying their revolt to such extreme lengths that they may produce conditions which are just as bad as those which they have repudiated!

In the system of thought to which we give our allegiance, virtue, sanity and true spirituality lie in the point midway between the extremes. All material things are, we believe, just as good, just as "holy" as are spiritual things. There is no external enmity between spirit and matter; they are the two poles of manifest existence, and it is in the *balanced use* of both spiritual and material principles that the way of progress lies. True spirituality, then, does not mean repudiation of the material world and all its affairs, repression of the material body with all its wonderful instincts and mechanisms, or concentration entirely upon your own fancied "spiritual development," ignoring all manifest duties to your fellow men. You cannot, of course, isolate yourself entirely, but you may so limit yourself by such an attitude that you cut down to a mere trickle the life-giving energies of the universe, energies that are essential for your healthy existence.

You may ask, what has all this to do with the development of clairvoyance? Of course, you may develop clairvoyant faculty without any religious or moral outlook in your mind; psychic faculties have nothing to do with moral or ethical rules. In fact, many of us, from long study of the subject, believe that some of the more pitiful offenders against the existing moral and ethical codes are as they are because, unknown to themselves, they are in some degree natural psychics, and are therefore open to telepathic pressures and temptations which the non-psychic does not usually experience. Therefore, without any religious or ethical standards, you may develop these psychic abilities, since they are in themselves natural powers just as are the physical senses.

Everyone possesses these faculties, but how near they are to emerging from the subconscious is another matter. With some people they are near the surface; with others they are so deep that the time which would be needed to bring them into the waking consciousness could well be applied to more effective fields of endeavor. Here an analogy may help. Let us take the case of two people, one of whom appears to have been born with a strong musical sense, the other having apparently no musical ability of any kind. In the first case, a comparatively short course of music lessons would show him to be a splendid musician, but the other person would probably be just as non-musical after twenty years of lessons, and the time he has wasted in this vain effort could have been employed to better purposes. So is it with the clairvoyant faculty. It is a natural power. If we seem to have over-emphasized this, it is because there is a mistaken idea abroad that these faculties are "gifts from the Gods."

Of course, in the end all life, all consciousness, all faculties, come from the Divine, but all work is manifest under immutable natural law. There is but one aspect of the universe which is supernatural and that is, to use an old phrase, the Holy One "Whom Natural hath not formed, from Whom all Nature proceeds and is governed." So our psychic faculties are natural powers. If we get this idea firmly fixed in our minds, which is why we have repeated it so many times, and if we choose our words so that we break away from the old forms of expression, then we will be less likely to get a wrong idea of ourselves. We have not been singled out by divine power to receive something unique, but are simply in the position of having become aware of another level of perception. It has nothing to do with our personal character, neither is it in any way a substitute for religion. So we should not be unduly boastful because we have the faculty in working order, neither should we fall into the error of believing that the possession of it shows our high spiritual development. It should be pointed out, however, that the range of our psychic powers does depend upon our moral development; we can only receive that which we can tune in to.

3

Training Techniques

AS in any science, art or craft, there are certain ways of proceeding, certain techniques which must be followed if we would succeed in our efforts to develop clairvoyance. Now the great trouble with the whole subject of psychic training in the past has been its involvement with various religious and cultural ideas. We do not mean to suggest that all these conditions and involvements were without their uses; indeed many of them have been of great assistance. However, there are certain essentials and these are what we want to deal with in this chapter. If you find that it helps you to cultivate your powers within the framework of some religion or philosophy, well and good. But do not acquire the habit into which many fall, and look with disdain or disapproval on those who find it possible to do without any such religious or philosophical assistance.

The clairvoyant faculty is an entirely natural power, and has nothing to do with moral, ethical or religious teaching, any more than our ordinary eyesight depends upon whether we belong to the Catholic Church or to the Hindu religion. It follows, then, that the singing of hymns and the use of various forms of prayer are not, in themselves necessary. At the same time, if such practices are real to us, if they have a definite meaning to us, then they can be of the greatest value. Indeed, in the deeper levels of development, prayer assumes a power and reality of

37

which we were not hitherto aware, and we then realize what a tremendous help it can be.

At the start of our development, we are dependent upon aids of all kinds, but as we progress we find that we can do without many of them. A little careful study of the lore that has come down to us concerning the development of the psychic faculties soon shows that much of it comes from the curious religio-magical traditions of the Middle Ages, much is derived from a very ancient folklore, and a certain amount from the continued experiments of many would-be scryers, as the clairvoyants are sometimes called. We can safely forget the magico-religious tradition, since it is not essential to the development of clairvoyance.

We can also dispense with a good deal of the folklore regarding clairvoyance. Some of this is based on old wives' tales, and has no basis in fact. The old wives *did* preserve and hand down some very important instructions, and these we can adapt and use today. Unfortunately, they handed down a good deal of foolishness and superstitious practice as well, and some of this is still with us. Now we come to the accounts which have been given us by those who have personally undertaken the task of clairvoyant development, and here again, their statements are colored by their individual temperaments. We have tried to include only those parts we consider to be of the essence of the matter.

Some of you may feel that we have left out a very important source of information on this subject: the instructions by various oriental "Swamis," "gurus" and "Rishis." We have done this deliberately. Having a fair working knowledge of some practical personal experience of these Eastern systems and of their methods and the results produced, we are firmly convinced that the exercises and teachings to be found in many of their books can be both misleading and harmful. For their safe and effective use, such methods depend upon the personal supervision of a guru or teacher who knows what he is doing, and can observe the results of these exercises in his *chela*, or pupil. When this can be done, then the Eastern method can be safely tried, although even under these conditions it may be found that the very different psychological outlooks of East and West introduce some difficulties and complications.

Having cleared some of the ground, we will repeat what we have already said about the basis of development. We think, then, of our consciousness as being divided into three parts. These are the waking consciousness, the subconscious and the superconscious. We may also consider the subconscious under two aspects: the *personal aspect* of the subconscious, and a far deeper and more extensive level which we share with all sentient life on this globe. This deeper level is the Collective Unconscious described by the great psychologist Dr. C. G. Jung and his followers. If we consider these two aspects of the mind then psychic development consists in building up certain links between the normal waking consciousness and the personal subconsciousness. Owing to the conditions under which human consciousness has evolved, there is a barrier, or division, between these two aspects of the mind, and the links which psychic development forms have to pass through this barrier in order that the results of the inner clairvoyant perception may be able to rise up into the waking consciousness.

These results come through in various ways, though it is probable, indeed tradition has always maintained this, that there is but one psychic sense of perception. But just as all our five physical senses are modifications of the basic physical sense of touch, so the psychic faculties of clairvoyance, clairaudience and clairsentience are modifications and expressions of the one basic psychic perception.

Your success in developing clairvoyance depends upon your bringing through the psychic perceptions in a visual form. If you were trying to develop clairaudience, then you would be trying to bring through this perception in subjective sounds and words. Much of the hard work of development as a clairvoyant is cut out if you have the natural power of *visualization*, or if you have trained yourself to visualize, to build up clear images in your mind. Some people have this power of mental visualization in an extraordinary degree. We remember meeting, many years ago, a girl of between five and six years of age who had an uncanny power to draw clear outline pictures of various kinds. When we asked her how she did it, she said, "I think, and then I draw a line round my think!" Rosalind Heywood, in her book *The Infinite Hive*, mentions this same power as used by her son in his schoolwork. This power to project a mental image so strongly as to see it apparently outside one's head is possessed by many artists, and, unfortunately, a certain type of mentally disturbed person often finds it happening involuntarily. Because such involuntary visions and voices are common symptoms of such mental trouble, all the more serious schools of thought on this subject insist upon their pupils never allowing this involuntary projection to take place. Incidentally, repeated investigations have shown that in some cases which have been diagnosed as purely mental illness, there was a true psychic element, and some of what certain of these people saw in visions was really due to clairvoyant perception.

The psychologist Freud, writing to Dr. Ernest Jones, said that if he had his time over again he would study psychic research, and Carl Jung did take a very active interest in it.

Should you find that your ordinary way of thinking is not along visual lines, then you will have to train yourself in conscious visualization. Here we may give you a hint which will save you a great deal of unnecessary trouble. Many of the books on the subject of visualization recommend the beginner to take a geometric form, such as a circle, a square or a triangle, and attempt to build it up in "the mind's eye." This can be done, but it is much easier, and just as effective, to use a picture containing numerous different details, such as a "mandala," for the mind can then move from point to point in the picture, gaining visualizing power and at the same time not becoming bored. It is this mental boredom which is possibly behind the gradual deterioration of the guesses made by Dr. Rhine's subjects with the Zener Cards which he uses. It has been noticed that a subject who has been accurately predicting the cards will gradually begin to lose the ability, and it is possibly this boredom which is responsible.

Incidentally, you may find that you remember a scene or object by means of what appears to be a mental "running commentary" upon it. Instead of seeing in your mind's eye a patch of color, you will simply have the word describing the color appearing in your mind. If this is the case, don't worry about it, but carry on attempting to improve your visual power. One of the beauties of this training in visualization is that you can do it at any convenient time, and you will find that such practice greatly increases your awareness of your surroundings, a power that can be of great value in ordinary life.

We will suppose that you are naturally or by training a good visual percipient, and can build up clear visual images. You can either keep these pictures inside your head or outlined against the dark screen of the closed eyes, or you may project them outwardly and see them apparently on the surface of a crystal, mirror or other such device. Much stress is laid by some authorities upon the use of a crystal or showstone. It must be of rock crystal, though one made of glass is allowable. (Actually, crystals made of transparent plastic are on sale!) It must be magnetized by the user, employing a certain magical ceremony; it must be wrapped in silk and kept away from strong light, and sometimes the advice is that the crystal be set in a frame of ebony on which have been painted in gold the twelve signs of the Zodiac. Others teach that it should be dedicated to a particular spirit. All this advice, in the form in which it is usually given, can be very misleading. There is, however, a definite reason for these instructions. Let us try to·rewrite the above list in another way. When we pick up and examine this crystal which we have bought, the examination of it links it in our minds with ourselves and with the purpose for which we bought it. If we have a definite intention to use it for certain types of clairvoyant work, then we have dedicated it to a particular "spirit" (for the spirits were said to rule over particular phases of the work; the "spirits of Mars", for instance, ruled over martial happenings, the "spirits of

Mercury" over intellectual things). In order to prevent psychic and mental confusion through the thoughts and emotions of others who might see the crystal in our possession, we keep it covered up and out of sight.

We are not saying that there are no other psychic reasons for all these instructions. They are part of a much greater setting in which crystals and showstones and mirrors played, and still play, their part, but for our present purposes they are not necessary. Those who, like ourselves, are born ritualists, and who find in ceremonial work a great aid to concentration may do all that is recommended in these instructions, but those to whom such methods are distasteful may adopt the purely mental approach we have indicated.

So far we have been referring to the crystal. But suppose you cannot afford to buy a crystal, what can you use? You need not worry, for there are substitutes that can be just as effective, or even better than the crystal. Some of these are:

1. The sand disc.
2. A sheet of white card with a large black disc painted in mat black paint in its center.
3. A black mirror.
4. A black bowl, shallow and half-filled with ink or other dark fluid.

To make a sand disc, take a sheet of stout white card say 7 in. x 7 in. square, and with a compass draw a circle of 5 in. diameter in its center. Carefully coat the inside of the circle with ocergum (not the modern resin glue), and while the gum is still moist, sprinkle fine sand on it. It need not necessarily be sand, any crystalline colored powder may be used. When dry, brush off any powder that has not adhered. This sounds very easy, but a certain knack is needed, and you may find several attempts necessary before you have made a disc to your satisfaction. The sand disc has one rather helpful property: it does away with the vague reflections which are usually given by the crystal and mirror. These reflections of surrounding objects can be very distracting to many people, though to others they become focusing points around which the visions form.

The black disc on a white ground can be made very simply by drawing a circle on a large sheet of white card, as described in the instructions for the manufacture of the sand disc. The circle is then painted black. One of the felt-tip pens now easily obtained from the stationer's can be used.

The black mirror is fairly easy to make. We have one which is very effective, and which was manufactured in the following way:

From a watchmaker or clockmaker obtain a circular "clock-glass." This is a convex glass cover used on clock-faces. Its diameter should be about 3½ in. though, of course, you may have it any diameter you like, within reason.

Now paint the convex side with black paint or enamel. You will find it best to give it two coats, allowing the first coat to dry thoroughly before applying the second. The next thing is to get something on which to mount the mirror. If you are good at wood-turning, or have a friend who is, it is possible to make a shallow bowl into which your mirror may be set leaving a frame of about one inch width around it. This frame you can stain or paint as you prefer, but we would advise you to use a subdued color, not a brilliant red or yellow! You may, if you like it, paint it with gold paint. It is even quite effective to mount the mirror in an old furniture polish tin; our own is so mounted in a tin which measures just over 3½ in. inside diameter. We supported the glass on a plaster of Paris ring. Incidentally, we once, many years ago, paid out very good and hard earned money for a black mirror, and it came duly mounted in a metal case inscribed with the signs of the Zodiac in gold. However, the mirror fell out of its case one day, and we found that the interior was also inscribed: "Cherry Blossom Boot Polish"! We have given this instance as it adds to what we have already told you, that the crystal, the mirror, the disc, have no intrinsic power in themselves, at least as far as we are concerned. They are simply "autoscopes," methods by which the psychic perceptions may be brought through the subconscious levels of the mind up into the waking consciousness. We have not troubled to describe the last method, the bowl of dark fluid. The ink pool is a method used in the Middle East. It is quite effective, though again you may get distracting reflections from its surface and, things being what they are, there is an occupational risk: spilled ink!

As a footnote, we may say that one of the most brilliant clairvoyants we ever met developed his clairvoyance by using a circular black-japanned tea tray, hung up on a wire. Judging by the results, it certainly worked well.

There are certain conditions which have to be taken into account when you decide to sit for clairvoyant development. The first of these is the state of mind in which you begin your work. It is not necessary that you should be a believer in all the myth and legend which has grown up around the subject. It is quite permissible for you to feel skeptical about the whole thing, but it is not helpful if you approach the subject in the spirit of the dying atheist who is reported to have prayed: "Oh God— if there is a God—save my soul—if I have a soul!" In Scottish law there can be a verdict of Guilty, or Not Guilty or Non-proven. If you enter upon your clairvoyant development prepared to accept whatever comes, and then to work it out in the way indicated, then much that you will feel at the beginning must be placed under the heading of "non-proven" may later be found to be suitable for either the "true" or "false" compartments of your thinking. So we would advise you to enter upon this path of personal psychic knowledge with an open mind, not tied to any particular dogma, but just willing to await whatever results may be obtained. This attitude is very important, since it is under these conditions that your subconscious mind is most likely to allow the psychic impressions to come into your waking mind.

So much for your preliminary attitude of mind. The next important point is the question of *records*. If you are going to do serious work in this field, it is essential that from the earliest sittings you keep a detailed record of everything that happens at each sitting. It most probably will be that for many sessions you will get little or nothing, but this should not prevent you from keeping records. Whatever clairvoyant visions may or may not present themselves, there are other details that should be logged. They will probably help you to find out why, at certain times, you get strong clairvoyant impressions and at other times you get nothing at all.

Those of us who have used the clairvoyant faculty for a long time, have found that there is a curious correlation between the phases of the moon and the activity of the psychic faculties. During the waxing phase of the moon, they appear to operate more easily under the control of the will. During the waning phase, although they may appear, they are often in chaotic and unfinished forms, and no longer appear to be under the full control of the will. For this reason, the experienced clairvoyant tends to look with a somewhat suspicious eye upon the psychic impressions received during this period. There are ways by which he can judge them, but these are peculiar to each person, and are the results of a fairly lengthy period of trial and error. Gradually you learn to evaluate the impressions you receive but, as we will try to describe shortly, there is also a very real, though subtle difference between the visions which come, as the ancients said, through the Gates of Horn, and those which emerge through the Gates of Ivory.

It is probably unnecessary for us to tell you that you are not likely to obtain good results if you have had a violent quarrel with someone just before the sitting, but you will also find that there are recurrent moods that seize you, and that can help or hinder your development. It is wise, therefore, for you to enter in your record the moods that affected you just before, during and after the sitting. After you have gone some months on the path of development, you will probably find that it all ties up with the moon's phases and can look back over the record of that period. It is also helpful if you make a note of the prevailing weather conditions, as these are important. All the foregoing points have an effect upon your mind and emotions, but now we come to those which affect your physical body. These are most important, for the sensations of the physical are so strong that they can, at the start of development, obliterate the faint impressions coming in through the subconscious and besides the "tone" of the physical body has a strong effect upon the mind and emotions.

The first and most important point is that you must be physically comfortable. Tight clothing, tight shoes, a very hard chair, the position of the crystal or other device which causes muscular strain, all of these must be right if you are to have complete bodily relaxation. The room should be comfortably warm, but not stuffy. The temperature that should be maintained varies with each individual, but normally should not be below 60°F. This is, of course, a matter of individual preference.

Only a light meal should be taken before the sitting; gazing at a crystal immediately after a substantial dinner will induce sleep, not psychic impressions! After the session, a light meal will be very helpful, as it tends to close down the psychic activities and restore you to normal consciousness.

Where you will sit for development depends upon the room available, if possible a special room set aside for this purpose. However, this is not necessary so long as it is possible for you to sit quietly and without any disturbance for the period of your session. Some people make an elaborate sanctuary into which they can retreat, and where they can employ whatever aids they feel necessary. In such a sanctuary, it is possible to use such aids as pictures that have some symbolic significance and incense, which also has its value. The latter has both a symbolic and psychological value, for by the mental law of association of ideas, the incense suggests a different atmosphere to that of everyday life. If it is used only during the sittings, then it becomes associated in the mind with this activity, and when you enter your sanctuary and light the incense, then the mind begins automatically to concentrate itself upon the object of the sitting. However, if a separate sanctuary is not available, we suggest that you do not use incense; it is not essential. One thing must be remembered in connection with this whole subject of development: all the aids that you may use at the start of your training must eventually be dispensed with, so that when the faculty is fully developed you must be able to use it under all normal conditions. The clairvoyant who is dependent upon a certain special set of circumstances before he can exercise his gift has limited himself by this dependency upon outside things.

The lighting should be dim. Some use a red light, some a blue one, while others simply dim or shade the ordinary white light. Again, it is an individual matter; choose that which seems best for you. The light must be low, however, so that surrounding objects are only dimly perceived. Later in your development you can increase the light, but at first it is best that you should have as little distraction as possible from chance reflections in the mirror or crystal.

The crystal, or other speculum as these things are sometimes called, should be so placed that the surface can be gazed upon without any strain. Eye strain should particularly be avoided, since this might well produce some adverse effects. The crystal is usually supplied with a small black stand, but if you wish you can simply cradle it in the folds of a piece of black velvet. It is best to place it on a small table so situated that you can gaze quietly and without strain at its surface.

All these conditions are external to you; how about your internal conditions? The chief mental condition should be one of quiet intention to sit for the development of clairvoyant power. The emotions should be as little disturbed as possible, and the physical body must be thoroughly relaxed. This last condition is far too often overlooked, but it is one of the essential prerequisites for development.

There are various methods of bringing about this relaxed physical condition, but the exercise we are now about to give you is, in our estimation, one of the best.

Sitting with the spine straight, breathe in deeply

through the nose. To do this, start from the diaphragm and then expand the rib-cage until a really full breath has been taken. The shallow chest, or upper-chest, breathing doesn't really do what is needed. As you breathe in, transfer your attention to the top of your head. Now slowly breathe out, and as you do so, mentally relax first the muscles of the scalp, then the face muscles, and then in turn the arms, trunk and legs, right down to the toes. Repeat this a set number of times. We suggest that you take six such deep breaths. You will find that at first you will tend to tense up again automatically as soon as your attention has passed from one point to the next, but soon the subconscious will obey your will and produce the required relaxation.

You are now ready to take your first step in the development of clairvoyance.

4

Vision

HAVING dealt as fully as possible with the general theory and conditions of clairvoyant development, we now come to the actual practice of scrying in the crystal or mirror. We will assume that you have carried out the instructions we have given you, and are now sitting in a thoroughly relaxed state of mind and body, gazing quietly and without strain at the surface of the speculum. For our purpose, let us suppose that it is the black mirror that is being used.

At first all that appears to happen is that the surface of the mirror gradually moves out of focus, and you cannot see it very well. Then, quite suddenly, it comes back into sharp detail. This may happen during part or even through the whole of the sitting at your first few attempts. You may also become aware of certain bodily sensations. These usually take the form of what appears to be a tight band round the forehead, and a curious itching or tickling sensation between the eyes, at the root of the nose. This tickling is referred to in some Eastern books as "the tickling of the ant," and this seems an apt name for it. It *does* feel very much as though some little insect was crawling around under the skin. These two happenings, the shifting focus of the eyes and the tight band with the tickling sensation, both seem to be due to purely physical causes, at least at the start of training. The disappearance and reappearance of the mirror is due to the muscles that control the focus-

49

ing of the lens of the eye becoming tired. As they relax, so the object at which you have been looking drops out of focus. Then, after a while, they tighten up and refocus on the object before them. The tight band and the tickling are due to slight changes in the circulation of the blood in the forehead, though the "tickling of the ant" indicates that a little-known aspect of the pituitary gland is being brought into activity. Do not be discouraged if this is all you experience in your first few sittings, these psychic impressions have to cut their new channel between the subconscious and the waking mind.

If you persevere, other signs will appear. One of the most usual is that the surface of the mirror seems to gradually cloud over, until it is as though you are looking at a curtain of grey mist which covers its whole extent. Then this curtain of mist may begin to break up and to whirl around in smaller clouds, and brilliant sparks of light flash out all over the mirror. At this stage you are likely to throw back your development by becoming excited over the fact that you are seeing something. This excitement can very effectually destroy the quiet poise of your mind, and so interfere with the tenuous lines of connection which are being built in the depths of the subconscious.

However, if you can keep your mind in the quiet state, then the appearances in the mirror may begin to increase and to take other forms. Fragmentary glimpses of brilliantly colored landscapes, faces grave and gay, and luminous colored clouds may all show themselves, but you will find that it is difficult, at first, to hold any one picture for more than a second or so.

When these landscapes, faces and colors appear, it is evidence that certain psychological changes are taking place in your mind, and it is these changes that will enable the inner vision to be brought to your waking self. These pictures are the first cousins to those curious little pictures which are seen by some people during the entry into sleep and again when awakening. The psychologists call them hypnogogic images, and assume that they are made and projected by the subconscious. This is. true enough, but in our present case they may be more than just images; they may be message-carrying images, bringing information that has been received by the inner senses. They are, as it were, waking dreams, and have their own definite meaning.

When you have reached this stage, you have begun to develop clairvoyance. You will discover for yourself the curious trick of holding the mind in a poised and yet relaxed condition, something which seems impossible at first. Many times you will become suddenly excited at what you see, and the whole vision will disappear immediately. You will also find that your visions begin to divide into two distinct groups. One will be much larger than the other, and this may indicate what type of vision you are developing. One set of images will be of normal everyday things, and the other will present symbolic forms to you. You will also find that the symbolic vision seems to be associated with a positive questioning attitude of your mind. The literal vision appears to be reflected into your mind without any effort on your part; it is a passive vision.

Some will tell you that the passive vision is to be avoided, but this is not necessarily valid. Whether you discern passively or actively, your gift can be of help to you and to others.

Having succeeded in seeing in the mirror, don't be in too much of a hurry to give a meaning to everything you see therein. A Catholic writer, the late Monsignor Robert Hugh Benson, referring to these visions, said that it was as though you were in a room with a window looking down on a busy street. The window blind is down, so that you cannot see out at all. Then quite suddenly, the blind is pulled aside for a second, and you are looking down at the crowded street and, in that momentary glimpse, you see a girl in a red dress carrying a basket of flowers. Then the blind cuts off your vision again. You would be very foolish if you began to argue that the girl was in any way concerned with you; she simply happened to be passing when you looked out. So it is with a great deal of this kind of

51

vision. We have spent many hours, during sleepless nights, in watching these vivid pictures in the astral light, without any reason to think that they were in any way connected with us personally. There are certain psychic currents that flow daily around this planet; the Hindus call them the *Tatvas,* and in each of the five types of *tatvic* current one kind of image appears to predominate. However, that will not directly concern you at the beginning of your development.

There are images, however, which are directly connected with you. They are images that are being used by your subconscious mind as a code by means of which certain information can be passed through to you. This information may relate to your own personal inner life and conditions, it may be definite information regarding others, information which your inner senses have received, or, in some cases, it may be due to the action of other minds that are passing a message through your inner self into your waking self in this way.

As you proceed with your development you will find that certain images have a symbolic value, and are the code that your inner self is using. You will have to learn from your visions what such symbolic forms *mean to you.* We have stressed these words for they are very important. What a symbol means to the inner self of one person is not necessarily the meaning it has for another. To us, the symbol of a cat seen in a vision has to do with Egyptian things, but a friend who was a very fine clairvoyant found that whenever he saw a similar symbol, it foreshadowed his being ill within a couple of days. He was engaged in lecturing work all over the country, and this recurring vision often enabled him to write cancelling a lecture engagement in time for those concerned to engage a substitute lecturer!

Here we come to something very important. These symbols, if you see them in a vision, will be found to be of two different kinds. One is seen in a vision without any emotional atmosphere, with no clue as to what it might mean. The second type is not only seen, but brings with it definite knowledge as to its meaning. This knowledge, which comes immediately with the vision is, in our experience, almost invariably correct. If you see a symbol and have to stop to interpret what it might mean, be wary, for your interpretation might be far from the real meaning. Incidentally, when you begin to get a succession of such symbols that you have to interpret for yourself, it is usually a sign that for one reason or another your clairvoyant powers are not working correctly, and you should give them a rest for a time.

There is another point with which we must deal, as we are considering the question of symbols. It applies mostly to those symbols that are interpreted as foreshadowing the future. Many times we have heard clairvoyants saying, "I see a lovely bunch of daffodils above you and this tells me that when the flowers are blooming in the spring, you will have good news," and so forth. Apart from the fact that flowers bloom long before spring, and that spring covers quite a few weeks, the whole thing is so indefinite that as a supposed clairvoyant impression of the future it is pretty futile. If the prediction cannot be narrowed down to less than a three-month period, then as a prediction it doesn't rate very highly. In any case, such vague descriptions strongly suggest that the clairvoyant ability of the person is very poor.

We suggest, therefore, that you train yourself to understand the symbols your inner senses present to you, and also that you endeavor to give clear and definite descriptions, rather than vague generalities. This can be done, but it does mean hard work. However, the results do justify the labor.

When you have gained the power to see the visions you have accomplished half your task. The next highly important thing you must do is to gain the power to shut off your visions. There are far too many half-baked clairvoyants wandering around; people who have begun to open up their psychic sight and then, for one reason or another have never mastered it. They have become involuntary seers, at the mercy of every psychic breeze that blows, and responsive in an automatic negative manner to all kinds of thought currents from those around them. Because of this, their clairvoyant ability, which could have been a great asset to them, becomes instead a liability. This can become a really dangerous matter; it is obvious that if you're crossing a busy street, you don't want a sudden vision of the Elysian Fields to appear. It might lead to an early residence in the superphysical world.

We advise you, therefore, to train yourself to keep the two levels of consciousness apart after you have had your sitting. Close down the clairvoyance by a calm effort of will. This does not mean that you need to grit your teeth and thrust out your jaw or go red in the face in a violent physical effort. To do this is a waste of energy, and is something akin to switching off the electric light by knocking up the switch handle with a sledge hammer. It may possibly put out the light, but it will almost certainly damage the switch. All you need to do is to quietly tell yourself that you are now finishing the sitting, and closing down the psychic faculty. Then immediately do some normal physical world activity, such as entering your record of what has happened during the session. If at any time afterwards the clairvoyant sense begins to show itself against your wishes, then at once turn your attention away from it. This must be done immediately or you will find that, as the vision forms before you, it will become increasingly difficult to shut it out. You may perhaps feel that if there is a possibility of something harmful happening to you, it would be helpful if a clairvoyant vision could suddenly warn you of impending trouble. This is so, and it can be so arranged that, by a definite mental suggestion that you give yourself, the clairvoyant power will begin to work when anything is likely to happen that may be to your detriment. These involuntary activities of the psychic senses are not to be encouraged unless, as we have said, some definite mental suggestion has built up the channel through which they can emerge into consciousness.

We have already suggested that it is advisable for you to keep silent about your development until you have both unfolded the power and learned to control it. Even then, you will find that if it is known that you have clairvoyant ability, you will be pestered by foolish people who simply desire to see some new thing, or who hope to gain something for themselves. Many of these people, who could well afford to pay for the services of a professional psychic, will see in your gift a splendid chance of getting something for nothing!

This brings us to the thorny question of professional psychism. Is it allowable to use this faculty for the purpose of earning a living? As the clairvoyant faculty is an entirely natural power, and not in itself sacrosanct, there is no logical reason why it may not be so employed. However, there are other considerations that must be taken into account. The clairvoyant is to a great extent an artist rather than a technician. His powers are variable, depending upon his inner personal conditions, as well as on outside factors. Until he has fully stabilized his power, he is not in a position to act as a professional psychic consultant, for he can never tell when the faculty will be available. Later he may be able to take upon himself this very demanding and responsible role, and by maintaining a high ethical standard, can be of great assistance to many people.

Finally, we may say that during some fifty years we have exercised the clairvoyant faculty without making any charge for our work, and have found a real and lasting satisfaction in the help we have been able to give to many people. We did, for some three weeks, break our rule and accept payment, but that time was sufficient for us to realize something of the temptations and difficulties that the professional psychic, if he be genuine, encounters.

5

A Word to the Wise

IN this section we have tried to give a simple and fairly clear outline of clairvoyant development, but we would ask readers to remember that it is only an outline. For instance, we have not gone into the symbolism and meaning of the colors which you will perceive clairvoyantly. This omission is because the whole question of color symbolism is somewhat confused; different "authorities" give different interpretations. As the inner mind of each seer tends to put its own meaning upon the colors and symbols it perceives, it is far better for the reader to learn by trial and error what the symbol code of his or her own inner self is, rather than try to impose the code of some other person upon it.

As you commence your training in clairvoyant perception you will very probably come into contact with others who are interested in the subject or who are themselves attempting such training. In one way this companionship with others who are treading the same path of development as yourself can be most helpful, especially if you are one to whom close human companionship is important. Much depends upon your temperamental make-up. However, such close companionship has advantages and disadvantages and you should consider very carefully whether your association is really necessary or helpful.

It may seem to you that we are trying to turn you into a cold-blooded and reserved being, intent only upon your own development. This is not so but, in this matter of psychic training and especially in its earlier stages, there are many who, far from helping you in your endeavors, will almost certainly interfere with them and slow down your development by their blundering activities.

In psychic training we find that telepathy is one of the many factors that we have to take into account. The unconscious telepathic action exerted upon you by others is a very real thing and may well hinder your development. For this reason alone it is not wise to allow too many people to know of your attempts at psychic training. Some may be ignorantly contemptuous of your efforts, and this critical contempt will be quickly picked up by your subconscious mind as your sensitivity increases. This will cause unnecessary strain on you.

It may also happen that you will be invited to join some group of people who are also interested in, or actually developing, psychic ability, and here you ought to be very careful indeed. Some of these groups and circles are connected with and work in, the general atmosphere of certain religious sects which have been built up around psychic phenomena. Others are linked with various occult fraternities, good and bad, and others again are based upon the use, or abuse, of psychedelic drugs. All these groups are usually eager to enlist new recruits, and if such recruits are already working with psychic things, then they are the more eagerly sought after by some of these groups.

There are two other points in connection with development in a group, and they are of the greatest importance to the person who is developing clairvoyance. First of all, membership in a group, though it may afford some measure of protection to the developing psychic during the earlier stages of his work, can very effectively hinder him later on. He may well find that when his clairvoyant ability has become more or less stabilized he has come up against the composite mind of the group, and this group-mind can very definitely limit the scope of his clairvoyance. In a group where the leaders are aware of this and take measures to counteract it, all will be well, but many groups clearly show that their leaders are "the blind lead-ing the blind." It is better to work on your own, even though you may crave the support and encouragement which a group can give, than to become the prisoner of a group-mind, however high sounding its claims may be.

Secondly, the clairvoyance developed in a group is somewhat of a hot-house plant as a general rule. Though it may work well in the group conditions it will tend to become intermittent and less reliable when used apart from the group. We have often seen this happen. These strictures do not apply, of course, to a well-run and disciplined group, but such groups are few and hard to find, so, as we have already said, work independently for quite a time until you feel that you can use your new faculty without its being influenced to any degree by the thought-currents of the group.

However, the effect of your clairvoyant development will probably cause you to begin to study the whole subject (of which this clairvoyant faculty is only one aspect), and this will bring you in touch with many of those organizations of which we have spoken. Such contacts should be avoided in the early stages of your development, but when your faculty has become stabilized and you have gone some way in the development of that virtue of discrimination of which we have spoken, you may begin to study these other aspects of development.

As soon as you begin to exhibit any clairvoyant power you will be besieged by people who want you to exercise your gift for them. In the first flush of successful development you may well fall into this trap, and exhaust yourself by attempting to gratify the appetite for wonders which is the real reason for these demands upon you. Then you may well find that the faculty begins to be erratic and finally ceases to function. You will then see how quickly these sensation seekers drop you and flock after another seer. We have seen it happen on many occasions, which is why we give you this warning against allowing yourself to be used in such a way.

It is all very well to develop clairvoyance, but the very next step you must take is to gain positive control over the new faculty. Not only must it not function without your conscious permission (except in the very exceptional cases which we have already mentioned), but it should be capable of being used without the need for any special conditions. In effect, you should be able to use it positively while you are standing on a busy subway platform, surrounded by noise and bustle. Such adverse conditions should not affect its working.

Now, you will probably be drawn into the study of the whole subject, and having stabilized your power it will be safe for you to investigate the various groups and societies which are concerned with the subject. You will soon discover that they make up a very mixed bag. Some of them you will find to be of a religio-philosophical nature, while others are sectarian religious bodies; others are devoted to occult philosophies of many kinds, some of which, as we have already pointed out, are best left alone.

Then there are those that deal with these subjects from the psychological and scientific angle, and the one common factor shared by them all is a hearty damnation of each other!

The literature on the subject you will find to be equally diverse. Some of the periodicals are house-magazines of the various organizations, others have managed to achieve publication by their own merit, and many more would never have achieved the dignity of book form if they had been forced to pass the scrutiny of a publisher's reader. This last remark does not mean that all that is privately published on these subjects is of no value. Sometimes a book which would have no commercial appeal, may have considerable merit, and deserves publication. In this case, private publication is helpful.

There are many other considerations, but you will find, if you keep a true and faithful record of all your sittings and all the results you obtain, that you will be able to understand in an increasing degree the wider aspects of your power. Do not forget, the "misses" as well as the "hits" must be recorded. Be honest with yourself, and your faculty will give you true information, but if you distort the knowledge you receive in this way, if you make false statements as to what you perceive, then your clairvoyant faculty will deteriorate and become unreliable. Remember, too, that you assume a very grave responsibility when you use these powers in your dealings with your fellow men. If, however, you begin and continue your clairvoyant career in the spirit which we have already indicated—the desire to know in order to serve—then you will find, as we found many years ago, that you will be led into a path of increasing service and increasing happiness.

More than this: to some of us who have developed the inner vision, glimpses have been gained of a mighty Will in the service of which is to be found true freedom and perfect peace.

So may it be with you who try this path of practical clairvoyant development.

PART II
Telepathy

6

What Is Telepathy?

"IT'S telepathy" is a common remark which is made when some curious happening in the mental field jolts the average person out of his usual thought habits, though the word is wrongly used in most cases. Let us therefore define this term "telepathy." The word comes from the early days of the Society for Psychical Research, which was formed in Victorian times to study these strange happenings which are now usually referred to as "supernormal phenomena." The Society for Psychical Research (hereafter termed the S.P.R.) is the prime source of what little material has been printed on the subject of telepathy. Three of the founders of the Society were Professor Sidgewick, Frank Podmore and F.H.W. Myers. Myers, who was a classical scholar and a poet of considerable merit, invented the name "telepathy," which is made up from two Greek words which together bear the meaning "feeling at a distance." This word was coined to cover all those reputed cases of super-normal activity that involve some kind of "action at a distance" between individuals. His own explanation of the word was that it was meant to cover "the communication of impressions of any kind from one mind to another, *independently of the recognized channels of sense.*"

This definition is broad enough to cover most supernormal phenomena, but he and his fellows in the Society coined a further term for this telepathic action and reaction when it was consciously exerted. This term was "thought transference," and we may simplify matters if we think of "telepathy" as the larger and more general field of "thought transference" in one particular aspect. As we shall see later, there are other specialized aspects to be dealt with, but for the moment we will use the word "telepathy" for both conscious and unconscious transference of thoughts, feelings and desires—and perhaps other things too. When the S.P.R. was founded, its investigators began to study the phenomena of telepathy and thought transference from two different angles. They collected many cases of the spontaneous manifestation of telepathy and checked them most carefully. At the same time, they began a series of carefully devised experiments in thought transference.

An International Reputation

It is not necessary, for our present purpose, to go further into the history of the S.P.R., except to say that it has established for itself an international reputation as a Society with a very high standard of scientific approach to all alleged super-normal happenings. Material processed by the S.P.R. is of high evidential value.

At the same time, it is to be noted that the Society as a whole has no definite official standpoint regarding super-normal subjects. Each member is free to make his own observations and to draw his own conclusions from the evidence submitted to him, but no one can speak in the name of the Society and say that this or that statement is the official opinion of the S.P.R. It is worth remembering this, for some members of the Society, by their eloquent and forceful statements in public, often lead unwary press reporters into stating that "The Society for Psychical Research says" thus and so.

Quite apart from the basic work of the S.P.R., many other experiments are conducted in this field. We even see the beginnings of official investigation in some of the

Communist countries. One extra difficulty for the Communists, dominated as they are by the dialectal materialism of Lenin and Marx, is that the phenomena must be brought within a purely materialistic frame of reference. For instance, does telepathy obey the law of inverse squares, as do all the known material energies? Apparently not, and so Iron Curtain experimenters must be at their wits' end to find some way of integrating telepathic phenomena into the general ideology of dialectal materialism.

There are others, not committed to any particular ideology, who are trying to find out how far the facts of telepathy increase or decrease the possibility of human survival beyond death. It is to be noticed that the *fact* of telepathy is no longer in doubt, except among a small group of die-hard "scientists."

Veneration of the Scientist

Of course, there is the general reaction of a large section of the public, which classes all such things as "A lot of—nonsense!" (Adjectives according to taste.) But even such uncompromising disbelievers, when approached in private, may admit that "there may be something in it, but the scientists will find it all out in time." This curious veneration of the scientist has in these days taken the place of the veneration which was once given to the priest. However, a "scientist" is one who uses a certain mental discipline in his researches, and anyone who uses this same method can equally claim to be a scientist. Briefly, the scientist observes the phenomena, forms certain theories to account for them, uses his theories to make repeated experiments, using different methods of approach, and finally puts forward the results of his experiments in the form of a hypothesis. This theory—for that is all it really is—will be closely scrutinized by his fellow scientists, and will quite possibly be considerably modified when they perform his experiments from the angle of their own particular outlook. Also, there are many scientists who, like many theologians, cannot accept new theories because they do not fit neatly into their own mode of thinking, and these people will do their best—or worst—to discredit both the theories and those who put them forward.

In all human thinking there is a tendency to fall into step with the majority, and every advance is instinctively resisted if it seems to go against what is already held. Not only is it resisted, it is often passionately resented, and the history of human thought shows only too clearly the depths to which even good men may sink. This is because of the tremendous power of the herd instinct within each one of us, making us emotionally biased against any new idea which might upset the established order of things. So human thinking tends to run in well-worn grooves, and this tendency, established through thousands of years, is not easily changed. But, as the professor in Oliver Wendell Holmes' book, *The Professor at the Breakfast Table* says quite correctly, a groove is the same as a grave, but not so deep. However, such a groove can become a grave —the grave of independent thought. All human organizations are liable to this, as history shows. It also shows there always comes a point when some people break away from such rigidity, whether it be scientific, medical, religious or ideological.

Super-normal Phenomena

At the present time, we see a great movement toward new ways of thinking, new outlooks on life and new methods of research into subjects that the orthodox institutions had previously dismissed with contempt. There is much foolishness, much credulity and much fanatical thinking about these super-normal phenomena. This applies not only to those who accept the possibility of psychic and occult happenings, but also to those in the other camp, who have a compulsive disbelief which refuses to consider any evidence and are equally fanatical in their denunciation and persecution of those who differ from them. However, these two opposing camps more or less cancel each other out, and can be left to fight the matter out in the light of their own prejudices. Here we are hoping to appeal to the open-minded and liberal thinkers at all levels, and to place before them certain information that will enable them to study this aspect of the super-normal in both a theoretical and a practical manner, in the true scientific spirit.

Many think of the instruments of the laboratory—the test-tubes, the Bunsen burners and the electrical gadgets—as being essential to the work of the scientist. This is only partly so, for all depends upon the kind of research the scientist is undertaking. All have their instruments, and some of these are very complicated. Others use very simple apparatus. Most workers in psychic science use very few such aids. The main instrument is oneself, though a number of recording devices of various kinds may be employed.

So far I have given the situation as seen from the scientific point of view, and this is an essential part of all our procedure if we are to produce results that will stand up to the searching criticism which will be leveled against them. Most people, however, do not worry unduly about the official scentific angle. They simply want to see for themselves if such a faculty as telepathy really exists, how it works, how it can be developed by the ordinary person, and to what use it may be put. Here we come into the sphere of moral values and judgments, for the telepathic faculty may, like all other gifts, be used or abused.

These introductory remarks are, we feel, sufficient foundation for a consideration of the general conditions under which telepathy works, and the varying forms it takes. Following on this, we will provide basic exercises required to bring the faculty into activity, together with helpful techniques. How much of the scientific method may be used in research is entirely under the individual's control. The more your work approaches scientific standards, the better will be the likelihood of having it accepted. In the author's opinion a middle of the road approach is best, for one can be far too rigid in this work. The subjects we use in our telepathic work are not inert chemical substances, nor mechanical instruments, though some of these may be used. Our principal instruments are living, thinking, feeling human beings, and this must always be kept in mind. Failure to recognize these personal elements has, in the past, often reduced or entirely inhibited any kind of result.

Changing Moods

Although the telepathic faculty is common to all, its development calls for unlimited patience—a quality which is not so common as it might be in this restless age. As has been said, our instruments are living, sensitive human beings; their mental and emotional states of consciousness are constantly changing, and thus varying the conditions under which our research is conducted. These changing moods are to be observed in both "sender" and "receiver." Above all else, however, there is required a state of mind which one famous Victorian scientist described as "being content to sit down humbly before nature, content to follow where she leads." Rigid conditions should be cautiously applied at the beginning of your work. Later, you will learn which conditions to tighten up, and which to relax. At the start, be mainly concerned with observed facts. The building up of theories follows at a later date.

When studying any new subject it is most foolish to ignore all that has been written about it. To start afresh without any previous data means that very little progress will be made; so what has been published upon the subject should be studied. It may well be that others, working along the same lines, have made certain suggestions as to further methods of approach, and these suggestions can give us a new insight. Again, others may have proved that certain lines of work lead to no real results, and this might prevent us wasting time following a cold trail. As we become more expert, it is possible to discover that some of these unproductive lines of research have value after all; the original researchers could have been at fault.

Here it is worth recalling that thousands of tons of pitchblende ore were thrown away as refuse because they did not contain the particular metal which was being sought. When Professor and Madame Curie worked on some of this refuse they discovered that one of the world's rarest and most important metals—radium—was contained in the pitchblende. A classic case of throwing away the baby with the bath water! It may, therefore, be interesting and possibly useful if, when we have established our results, we look back at some of these former experiments which apparently produced no results. It may well be that a new angle of approach will be found, and new facts unearthed.

It is always a great temptation, when starting to read on a subject such as this for the first time, to ignore the introductory chapters. Some actually boast of doing this. They want to get to the exercises, they want to get started. However, the introductory remarks have two important functions. One is to give you a good general knowledge of the subject, and the second is to link up this new knowledge with your own general knowledge. For this reason, these introductory remarks should be of value, as they condition your mind to practical work ahead.

7

Physical Conditions for Successful Experiments

IN any field of research it is always an advantage to be able to survey the area in which we are about to work, and this is doubly so when we are dealing with such a subject as telepathy. Although we may be ignorant of what is included in our field of research (except perhaps for some general outlines), we must always bear in mind the truth that no subject can be studied in isolation. Always, and in the most complex and indirect ways, it is linked with many other fields of human research.

Ethical Considerations

Before beginning to study the faculty in detail, it may be helpful if we look at it from the point of view of "motive." After all, we usually have some motive in starting out on a new path of work. What then is our motive in studying the telepathic faculty? One motive, of course, can be the simple desire to know. But it is not enough to investigate a matter; what do we do with our findings? Telepathy, like any other faculty of the mind, can be used for good or evil, for in itself it is neutral. Here we are coming into the area of ethics and morals, and we are plunged into a jungle of conflicting ideas, the widely differing mores or habits of life and conduct of the various tribes of our civilization. We may easily become lost in this moral-immoral-amoral jungle of thought and desire, unless we have some simple guidelines to which we can refer—some Ariadne's thread which will guide us through this moral maze.

Where our own interests are concerned, we naturally tend to oppose any new ideas which we feel may threaten our way of thinking. This way of thinking is far more widespread than the average person suspects, and in fact it underlies most of our thinking on any subject in which we have a personal interest. This opposition to new ideas is, of course, a purely emotional and irrational reaction. So any new idea has to face the irrational reaction of the mass of humanity: "It's only true if it has anything within it which is of use for me." Although this crude statement may be worded in several different ways, and under various face-saving and conventional phrases, it is the basic reaction of the vast majority of people. If we look carefully into our own personal motives for studying and using the telepathic faculty, we will almost certainly find this basic query lurking in some dark corner of our mind. Which, of course, simply means that we are all fallible human beings.

However, there are certain guidelines, and for our purpose they may be summed up in three brief statements. The first is that we must not attempt to use any telepathic power we may develop simply for our own personal gain. The second is that we should dedicate our new power to the service of God and man; we should desire to know in order to serve. The third is that under no circumstances at all should we use the telepathic power to *dominate any other person against their will.* We are fully aware that these are "counsels of perfection," and they are put forward as such. As a general rule we err and fall short of the ideal, but it is well to keep these counsels of perfection in the forefront of our thinking when we are dealing with all these super-normal matters.

The Aura

Around every person is to be found a very real field of psychic energy. It is commonly referred to as the "aura," and a good deal of foolish thinking has surrounded the subject. It is sufficient to say that the normal limits of the aura form a kind of psychic barrier, and we must not, by our telepathic practice, do anything to break down this personal barrier against the will of the person concerned. Should they voluntarily let down their defenses, then we may—if we are sure of our motives—affect them in a person-to-person telepathic manner. However, such agreement must not be obtained by any questionable method such as verbal suggestion (the person being "talked into" agreement), neither must any drugs be used or, and this is very important, the normal contact between friends or lovers be exploited in this way.

It is well to remember that just as natural laws exist on the physical plane, so there are similar laws on the psychic levels, and although on both levels of existence we may appear to break them, in the end it is very true that "as a man soweth, so shall he also reap." There is a true morality which does not merely govern the customs of the tribe, but recognizes a law of cause and effect that holds good on all planes of existence. As far as telepathy is concerned, we can say that there are certain basic considerations of moral responsibility to be taken into account. Anyone who infringes these will sooner or later experience the results of such foolishness.

General Conditions

We can now move to the general conditions that have been found best for telepathic work. The whole subject of conditions is a thorny one. Many so-called scientists insist upon imposing their own rigid conditions upon any experiment that they may deign to make in this field, totally overlooking the fact that these conditions may prevent anything super-normal happening.

If, when we were taking a photograph, some member of a Stone Age tribe of savages should insist upon removing the film from the camera and examining it in broad daylight before allowing us to take the picture, our efforts would be entirely wasted, since the film would have been ruined by the very same power of light which, under correct conditions, will give us a perfect photograph. Our annoyance when our Stone Age friend joyfully proclaimed that photography was a fake, would be closely paralleled by the similar annoyance felt by experienced investigators of psychic phenomena who encounter the same Stone Age mentality disguised as "scientific conditions." It is better, therefore, not to impose too rigid conditions in the early stages of your work. As you progress in your experiments, you will be able to discover the conditions which are necessary. These conditions will vary from one individual to another, but a general pattern will emerge, and this will indicate to you which conditions should be relaxed and which tightened up.

Although it is convenient to use the terms "sender" and "receiver" for the two people concerned in a telepathic experiment, we have found by experience that although on the outer levels this is true enough—the sender has the image to "send" and the receiver is supposed to pick up that image and record it—the inner processes are somewhat different. It would appear, from many experiments, that in the majority of cases the receiver, far from being a passive mirror of the images "sent" by the sender, actually reaches out in the inner consciousness and makes a positive contact with him, thus receiving the image which is being held in the sender's mind.

The ordinary radio analogy is not applicable in this form of telepathic transference. There are several levels of telepathic transference that may come into play, and this brings an element of complexity into the work. It is here that we find a curious fact. When the sender thinks of the receiver as being some distance away, the results are limited by his ideas as to that distance. If, however, he strongly pictures the receiver as being close to him, then the results obtained are significantly better. This appears to suggest that the occult teaching that distance on the inner levels is a matter of sympathy, and has little to do with any physical ideas of distance, may very well be true. In any case, for the sender to work as if this were true seems to improve the results obtained.

Telepathic Training

Here we come to the question of telepathic training. So many who try to work in this field appear to think that the telepathic faculty is something that does not need any training, but those who have gone into the matter more deeply realize that the faculty must first be aroused, then stabilized and carefully trained, if worthwhile results are to be obtained. There are certain methods of arousing the telepathic sensitivity, but generally speaking the desire to use the faculty will begin to arouse it.

Unconscious telepathic action is constantly at work around us, and this suggests that very little stimulus is needed to bring it into normal waking consciousness. But it must then be trained, otherwise it becomes what is sometimes termed a "wild talent," unreliable and uncertain in its action. In certain occult organizations, this training has become a fine art, and telepathy of an order seldom seen outside the Lodges has been developed and used, as I have seen. There is nothing particularly secret about the methods used by occultists. What *is* noticeable is the systematic training of both sender and receiver. It is perfectly possible for a group of people to transmit a combined message to a single person, and it is equally possible for one person to communicate with a group. I have seen both these forms of telepathy used, and have observed that it is the steady, disciplined work put into the training which gives results.

Now we must consider in greater detail the conditions under which our experiments should be conducted. First of all, we must come to our subject with at least some belief in its possibility. Our "belief" may amount to nothing more than a mental endeavor to be neutral in our approach to the subject. It is usually thought that it is necessary for the sender to "concentrate" for a fair length of time on the thought image to be transmitted. It is also thought that the sender should intensely desire to project the message from where he is to a place some distance away. This is not so. The period of time in which the sender is active need be only a fraction of a minute; indeed, hard concentration over a considerable period of time may actually prevent any thought transference.

The actual machinery of the telepathic faculty is in the subconscious level of the minds of both the sender and the receiver. All that is required of the sender is that he form as clear a picture as possible of the thought to be sent, together with the emotion connected with it. It is the lack of this emotional charge which so often causes the telepathic sensitive to fail. Realizing this, modern parapsychologists have begun to use images rather than the Zener cards and geometrical diagrams for transmission purposes.

Intention and Visualization

The charged mental image which has been built up by the consciously direct effort of the sender has now to be impressed upon his own subconsciousness under the best possible conditions. This brings us to the consideration of "intention" and "visualization." Intention, as we are using the word, is an act of will by means of which we switch on the subconscious mental machinery in readiness for the work at hand. It should be a *calm* exertion of the will; there must be no fierce effort involved. This is true in all the finer psychic phenomena, as well as in the routine training of concentration, meditation and visualization. There is a story told of the late Dr. Annie Besant's early days as the pupil of the theosophical genius, Mme.

H.P. Blavatsky. Dr. Besant was sitting attempting to concentrate according to the instructions given her by Mme. Blavatsky. Presently that lady quietly remarked, "My dear Annie, you do not concentrate with your eyebrows!" In this way she called Dr. Besant's attention to the fact that she was tensing the muscles of her face as she tried hard to concentrate.

Most beginners fall into this trap, which stems from the very close link between the mind and the body, whereby the body responds to the various mental and emotional tensions. There is a "language of the body" which automatically expresses this. In our telepathic work this amounts to a voice calling out just when we can do without it, and we have to take steps to silence it. This is done by training oneself in relaxation. There are many methods of relaxation, but the one we shall give you is very simple and effective. There is also a simple breathing exercise which may also help. Having attained the relaxed state the sender is ready to transmit the message to the receiver. We have said that there should be no straining to send the thought. All that is necessary is to have as clear a mental picture as possible. This picture can be built up by visualizing it clearly, meaning that the visualizing power must have been deliberately trained, for clear natural visualization is not so common. Usually, prepared pictures and images are used, but the work involved in training the visualizing faculty will give an extra clearness to the images which the sender has to transfer to his subconscious mind, and for this reason we strongly advise you to train the visualization faculty, even though you may perhaps have the visualizing power fairly well developed already, and be able to use it consistently.

Projected Pictures

There are people who are able to look at any plain surface, such as a sheet of paper, and project upon it a picture that they have visualized mentally, and this projected image will appear as an objective picture to them. Under certain conditions such projected pictures may be seen by other people who are looking at the paper upon which the visualizations have been projected. Here we have a shared telepathy, and many experiments have been made along this line.

This digression on visualization may seem to have broken the sequence of what I have been saying, but as the visualizing faculty is of such great importance in these matters, I feel that I am justified in reiterating to some extent the discussion of visualization in Part I.

To return to our sender. Sitting in the relaxed condition, and asserting his intention to transmit, the picture or image in his conscious mind will be imposed upon the sensitive subconscious levels of his mind, and will be open to the corresponding levels of the receiver's mind. From thence it will, when the conditions are right, emerge into his conscious mind and be recorded by him. We have said *when the conditions are right,* for there is a curious time lag which is often observed in this telepathic work. The message is received at the time it is sent, but for some reason or other, it is delayed, or totally suppressed. This has to do with the activities of the conscious mind of the receiver, but usually in experimental work there is a strong reason for the images to emerge as soon as received. How this is done is largely a matter of psychological type. It may be an inner voice speaking, or a visual image may be seen. Sometimes it comes as a clear and definite knowledge—without any image at all. Sometimes it may be a strong mental impression. Yet again it may not come into the receiver's conscious mind at all, but may emerge through what is known as "automatic writing." It may also happen that more than one channel may be used.

Case of Automatic Writing

In connection with the reception of telepathic messages by means of automatic writing, there are a good many actual cases of this which have been recorded in the annals of psychical research. W.T. Stead, the journalist and social reformer, who perished in the *Titanic* disaster, had the power of obtaining telepathic messages from others in this way, as did also Miss E.K. Bates, one of the early members of the S.P.R.; and there were many others who recorded their experiences of this form of telepathic reception. At one time I had the same faculty, and an example of my experiences may be of interest. At the time I was living some miles from London, where my teacher in these matters lived. Quite without any premeditation I followed an impulse, took pencil and paper, and prepared for automatic writing. To my surprise, I wrote: "I am in Switzerland, staying at a hotel high in the mountains. I am sitting on the veranda of the hotel, watching the sunrise on the snow peaks." This message was a total surprise, since I had not known that my teacher was out of town. To check on this I phoned his London address. The housekeeper answered and said that he was away on holiday in Switzerland. The next time I saw the teacher, I asked him about this message. He said that it was perfectly correct, but he had no conscious knowledge of having sent such a message. This was also the case of those friends of W.T. Stead who likewise communicated through my hand by this automatic writing. They, too, were ignorant of having sent any messages, even though these were factually correct. It would appear from this that some part of our inner consciousness may be very active in a supernormal way without the conscious mind knowing anything at all about it.

8

Psychical and Psychological Conditions

HERE we must return to the brief reference made in Chapter Seven concerning "distance." I said that if the sender transmitted the message with the thought that the receiver was quite close to him, it stood a better chance of being received. I shall now enlarge on this, for it makes a very considerable difference to the results we may get. We are used to regarding our surroundings as separated from us by space or distance, and, of course, normal life on earth could not be carried out if we were to ignore this factor of distance. The trouble is that we tend to project the idea of physical distance into the non-physical area in which we are conducting our telepathic experiments. We are used to thinking of ourselves as encapsulated beings—units of life that are separate from all other similar units—but experience in the use of the telepathic and psychic faculties soon convinces us that there are aspects of our inner nature that are always in some kind of actual contact with all other life units. This being the case, if we think of the receiver as being separated by distance from the sender, then the results we obtain will be affected by that belief, the idea of sending the message over a distance will cause us to think of it in terms of *limitation*, and we may inwardly doubt whether we can project our thoughts so far. The subconscious mind, ever willing to carry out the slightest suggestion from our conscious mind, will, therefore, respond by limiting the results of our experiment. If, on the other hand, we think of the receiver as being near us, then the subconscious will again oblige, and will not allow the impression of distance to interfere with the results.

The whole concept of "near" and "far" assumes a new form when we begin to be successful in our telepathic work, for we begin to think in a new way, with greater freedom from the physically limited thinking in which we usually indulge.

A Definite System

I have now dealt with the principal conditions that make for success in telepathic experiments. There are others, of course, which can do much to help or hinder us. The first of these conditions is that we should evolve a definite system of experimentation. All results should be noted down immediately after the experiment—nothing should be kept till later. The human memory is a fallible thing and we are apt, quite unconsciously, to alter the record unless it has been recorded on the physical level in some way. We are liable to stress certain points and to forget others—a fact that is daily demonstrated by witnesses in law courts and in police interrogations. Of course, if your experiments are made purely as an interesting study of what appears to be a super-normal happening, and you are not interested in giving any scientific evidence to the world, then you can dispense with many of the conditions we have suggested.

Some who have read so far may indeed feel that the subject has been made to appear far too complicated by what I have said, and that a simple procedure such as simply sitting down and willing the receiver to pick up the idea to be transmitted would produce results without the careful observance of all the conditions I have suggested. This may very well be—for some. However, what has been put before you is the result of many years' practical experience in this field of study.

Associated with the need for a definite system is another condition; not only should the actual experiment be recorded, but the physical climate should also be noted. Phases of the moon (as explained more fully in Chapter Three), atmospheric conditions such as cloud, rain, wind, and variations such as electrical tension in the air due to thundery conditions, should be noted. Psychic phenomena —and telepathy is a psychic phenomenon—are considerably affected by the subjective reactions of experimenters to atmospheric variations. For instance, there is a fairly definite variation due to the position of the moon, and all such details can introduce marked alterations in the working of the psychic faculty.

Outside Distractions

The immediate conditions of the experiment should also be noted. The warmth of the room in which the work is done, the absence or otherwise of outside distractions, such as loud or insistent noises (on occasion I have found the heavy ticking of a grandfather clock in the room distracted my attention), the form of the room, and last, but not least, the physical comfort of the experimenters— more especially the sender and receiver.

Finally, and this is most important, both the sender and the receiver should be emotionally calm; there should have been no heated exchange of views before the start of the experiment. This point is really important, for such emotional upset weakens the emergence of the psychic faculty, or, if it does manage to appear, it may well pick up and transmit the emotional ideas instead of the image which should have been sent. This will still be an example of telepathy, but not an example of controlled experimental work. We are not saying that such emotional telepathy is wrong, since most spontaneous telepathy has an emotional content. What we are saying is that in controlled experiments this emotion tends to interfere with the results.

One of the most important conditions of experimental telepathic work is patience! So many people who attempt to work in the field of ESP, telepathy and psychic phenomena in general, fail to realize that results are not, as a rule, obtained at the first sitting—or the fifth, and for this reason are apt to drop the whole subject in disgust. I heard it stated recently, "Telepathy? Oh yes, I've tried five experiments, but got nothing. I doubt whether it ever happens." What such people do not understand is that just as we have the physical organs of the senses, so it may well be that there are similar *super-physical* organs through which the mind receives, and reacts to, impressions derived from a super-physical source. The physical sense organs have evolved over millions of years, but perhaps the super-physical sense organs are not so highly developed. Here and there, however, and in an ever-increasing degree, people are emerging in whom these deeper senses seem to be active, and even though, in some cases, these senses do not normally surface in the waking mind, they need very little stimulus to do so.

Outer Psychic Conditions

Such people make the best receivers, and since the use of a faculty strengthens and widens its scope of action, these natural sensitives prove most useful. It is not always possible to say whether a particular percipient is telepathic, only repeated experiment will give this knowledge. One thing is clear, however, as we have found from long experience in this field; these people will be found to be particularly sensitive to the outer conditions we have mentioned: lunar, solar, atmospheric and emotional. This sensitivity to outer psychic conditions introduces an element of continual uncertainty as to results. Indeed, it may well prevent any experiment from being successful, until it has been controlled. It is very important that those who take part in these telepathic experiments should realize that both those who send and those who receive are human beings and are therefore liable to emotional reactions that can affect the success or failure of the experiments.

For this reason, we suggest that a series of perhaps ten experiments should be made without either sender or receiver being told of the number of "hits" or "misses." This will prevent their getting unduly depressed at the high percentage of misses common in the early stages of training. By using a unit of ten experiments at a time it is easy to check the percentage of successes and failures. Usually the latter is much greater, unless you have had the good fortune to get two people who are strongly sensitive, and who are emotionally compatible. This emotional sympathy is usually a sign of an inner psychic sympathy, or rapport, as it is termed.

We suggested that, if possible, a team of three or four pairs of senders and receivers should be chosen, and the various permutations be worked out until it is found which sender works best with which receiver. These two will constitute the first line of research. It must, however, be remembered that the faculty grows with use, so the other members of the team should be paired off, and act as senders and receivers in another set of experiments. Their percentage of failures may be greater than those of the first set of sensitives, but any faint telepathic reactions will be strengthened by practice, and a second team may be established. With time, the second team may well become very successful, and again, the value of patience is obvious.

Boredom Increases Failure

It has been observed by those who have studied the results of such psychic experiments as these, that the percentage of failures tends to increase when the subjects become bored. This is always an uncertain factor, since people vary greatly in their reactions. When the experiment has lasted too long, or for other reasons loses interest, the mistakes begin to pile up, until there is practically no success at all. If, however, the experiments are not carried on too long at any one time, and if the subject matter of the messages is made interesting, the percentage of successes begins to rise. When telepathic rapport between two individuals has been developed and stabilized, however, the percentages of success will normally increase, and with practice the experiments will become more or less independent of the emotional and other factors which formerly prevented their successful working. These adverse factors will never be entirely overcome, but they will not get in the way as they formerly did. Also, the way in which they affect the results will have been found, and can be allowed for in any experiment.

A "Picture Consciousness"

The subconscious mind is primarily a "picture consciousness" and responds far more readily to images of objects than to abstract ideas. By images we do not, of course, mean *visual* pictures alone, but include those which are built up by the other senses such as touch, taste, hearing and scent. If the message to be sent contains more than one of these sense pictures, it will have a much better chance of being recorded by the receiver. Whatever picture is used for the development of concentration, it should be as interesting as possible, and, like the messages of telepathy, should preferably include some of the "picture" produced by the other senses.

The same principle applies to telepathic transmission. An example would be if the sender was told to send a picture of a rosebush in full bloom. Not only should the visual picture be held in his mind, but also the scent of the blossoms, the crispness of the leaves, the softness of the petals, and the sharp prick of the thorns on the branches. The *visual* picture, which as a rule is the basis upon which the telepathic impression is based, can be transmitted more effectively if it is isolated from its surroundings.

84

Otherwise some of these surroundings may be transmitted unconsciously, and, not being included in the image it is desired to send, although they are received by the receiver, may easily be dismissed as of no consequence, and the experiment deemed a failure. In reality it may have been a decided success as far as telepathy goes, even though the intended picture was not received.

One method of isolating the picture to be sent is to use the artist's trick of putting the hands around the eyes so as to shut out all surrounding images except the one you require. Another form of this is to construct a hollow cardboard tube through which the picture is gazed at. I have found this method most effective.

In this chapter we have given you a fair idea of the psychical and psychological conditions that govern success-ful telepathy. There are others, but they affect the deeper levels of telepathic action, and will be referred to later. Incidentally, we may point out that, contrary to popular opinion, men as well as women may be receivers; sex has very little to do with the faculty, except that the feminine mind is, as a rule, more receptive. But there are many men who possess the same capacity and can be trained to be very efficient receivers.

9

Training for Telepathy

IN the last chapter I outlined the general conditions which govern telepathic transmission of thought. Now we will deal with the training required by both sender and receiver, together with a detailed description of the procedure used in telepathic work. It may puzzle some readers to find that "training" is required by all who take part in telepathic work. However, this is the case, for although we wrote of training being required by the sender and the receiver, it is important that all who are taking part in the experiments should have been trained to work as a unit, each contributing his own particular technique towards the final result. Thus the recorders at both ends of the experiment must follow a technique that enables them to give a true and scientific record of the proceedings.

Of course, as I have said before, it is possible—sometimes—to transmit telepathic impressions by simply sitting down and "willing" the message to be received. Equally, it is possible—sometimes—to simply sit down, make the mind a blank (which is a somewhat difficult achievement), and receive the projected message. It is equally possible for you to produce a true and scientific record of proceedings without having had any previous training, but this is not quite so easy as it sounds.

Sender and Receiver

So let us now consider the training of a sender, or "agent." Incidentally, he should also train as a receiver, and this dual training applies to the receiver—he should train to be a sender. Both types of training should be entered by each, so that they do not become biased in either direction. Equilibrium is the basis of the work. The dangers which lie in lopsided development are greater for the receiver than for the sender, since they may make him too sensitive and open to outside influences. Each method of training should be considered separately, though there is a fair amount of common ground. Let us briefly consider the basis of the training of the sender. The actual message is passed from the sender's conscious mind into the subconscious level, and the same mechanism is at work with the receiver, except that the message emerges from his subconscious into his conscious mind, save when true automatic writing takes place. In the latter case the message is passed by the subconscious into the motor centers and thence emerges in automatic writing. In both cases, the subconscious is the real agent in the matter, and what is required is to transmit the image from the conscious mind of the sender into his subconscious, on the one hand, and on the other to transfer the image from the subconscious mind.

Relaxation and Breathing Technique

It is necessary, therefore, to find some way of linking the two levels of the mind, so that there is an emergence of the subconscious—or a part thereof—into the conscious mind. This can be done by the use of a relaxation and breathing technique common to many esoteric training systems. The principle upon which these exercises work

87

is based upon the fact that in the ordinary person there is a continual state of stress, especially nowadays, and this results in an unwanted tension between mind and body. If the body can be relaxed, the mind will follow suit. Most stress is really emotional in nature, and the breathing and relaxation take account of this, for breath and the emotions are closely linked. If you wish to prove the truth of this statement, the following little experiment will help you.

When you are next in the middle of emotional stress, start breathing *slowly* in and out. (A slow count of five for the in-breathing, a count of two while retaining the breath, a count of five breathing out, and another count of two—this completes the cycle). If you continue this breathing for one minute you will find that the emotional feelings will have considerably diminished, or even disappeared. The principle is that you cannot feel intensely while breathing deeply and slowly. The Hindu yogis found out this fact many centuries ago, and certain breathing exercises were evolved, using this principle. Some of this exercises, being meant for Indian bodies, are not quite so helpful to many in the West, whose psychology and bodily development varies from those in the East. There are, however, Western equivalents to the Eastern exercises and the one we have just given works very well.

When holding the breath it is important to avoid closing the throat; use the chest muscles to prevent the rib-cage from collapsing back. If anyone were to tap your chest smartly while you were holding in the breath, the air would immediately be puffed out—there would be no check in the throat. This deep breathing, incidentally, gently massages the solar plexus, the nerve center connected closely with the emotions, reducing the stresses in it and thus weakening our involuntary emotional reactions.

Such reduction of nervous reaction affects the whole body, lessening muscular tensions. This reduction may be still further increased by using the following exercise. Sit quietly in a comfortable—but not too soft—

chair, and for one minute practice the breathing exercise we have given. Now fix your mental attention upon the top of your head and contract the scalp muscles. Let them relax and then move to your facial muscles. Contract them—especially those of the forehead—and then relax them. Pass down your body, contracting and releasing the muscles as you move mentally from your head to your feet. At first you will find that you tend automatically to resume the tensions, but with practice you will find that this will cease, and you will be able to rest in a totally relaxed condition. This is a most restful condition, and when you have succeeded in arriving at it and holding it without any strain, bodily or mental, you may take a further step.

The Conditional Reflex

Select any word or symbol that appeals to you, and link it with the feeling of quiet, peaceful relaxation which you have induced in yourself. Whenever you sound the word (either vocally or mentally), or visualize the symbol chosen, you will find the word or symbol immediately induces the relaxed condition. When you have managed to link the word or symbol with the relaxed state, then you will have mastered what is known as the conditioned reflex.

You can, of course, begin your telepathic experiments before you have fully mastered the exercise. The only difference is that you may have more successes and fewer failures in relation to your proficiency in the exercise, so the sooner you are able to master it, the better.

A Typical Experiment

Now for a detailed description of a typical well-planned telepathic experiment. First of all, the room or rooms used must be reasonably heated; not too hot and not too cold. Either extreme will intefere with the work. The chairs in which you sit should be comfortable—but not too comfortable. They should enable you to look at whatever picture you are going to try to transmit without any undue strain. The picture itself may be placed flat on the top of a table, or it may be held upright in a holder of some kind, such as those used by typists to hold documents they are copying. Solid objects may simply be placed on the top of a table. If the receiver is in the same room as the sender, some provision must be made to prevent the receiver from seeing the object or picture, and the best way to do this is to screen the table where the sender is seated. It might be helpful if the receiver was fitted with ear-plugs, which would prevent his hearing even the faintest whisper.

One person should act as recorder. His work is to supply the pictures, symbols, drawings or objects that are to be used in the experiments, and to make an accurate record of the time of each experiment, together with any relevant data, such as the atmospheric conditions, the temperature of the room, the lunar positions (new, full or waning), and any other detail that might affect the experiment. Foremost among these will be the mental, emotional and physical condition of the sender (and the receiver if they are both in the same room).

Should the sender and the receiver be in separate rooms, then a recorder should be with the receiver also, and should record the same kind of detail as for the sender. It is very important that there should be no unnecessary conversation in the room, and as far as possible, outside noises should be kept to a minimum. Of course, this latter provision is the ideal but it may not always be possible. But if we can get some quietness, it will help greatly.

Sub-vocal Speech

Whether the experiments take place in a single room or whether the receiver is seated in another room is really a matter of the availability of another room. If such a separate room is obtainable, it will help greatly, for it will prevent any possibility of the receiver picking up clues that may be given by the sender's "sub-vocal speech." This means that, quite unconsciously, the sender may speak of what he is sending, but so silently and automatically that he is totally unaware of doing it. The receiver, however, being in a sensitized condition, may pick up the very faint sounds.

In this connection, many experiments with mesmeric and hypnotic subjects have proved that a condition of "hyperaesthesia" or extreme sensitivity of the senses may be induced in the subject, and I have witnessed such cases, where mesmerized subjects could hear faint whispers at a distance of over fifty feet. This extreme sensitivity can often ruin a telepathic experiment, so it is as well if the sender is in one room, and the receiver in another. When this can be done, it is helpful if those who are acting as recorders in both rooms should synchronize their watches, so that the times of sending and receiving may be exactly noted. We have described the arrangements for the sender.

What conditions are required at the receiver's end? The same general conditions, such as freedom from noise and from bodily discomfort are required. In addition a writing pad or sheets of paper and pencils and pens for the use of the receiver to record any impressions should be provided. There should also be a recorder, if the sender and receiver are in separate rooms. Again, the room lighting should not be too strong, but there should be enough to enable notes to be taken.

The First Transmission

We will assume that the recorder has collected a number of pictures, symbols, drawings or small objects which are to be used in the experiment. These are kept by him, are not shown to anyone else, and are so arranged that only one article, picture or drawing can be used at a time. The room has been prepared, and everything is now ready for the first transmission. The recorder takes one picture, drawing, symbol or image and places it in front of the sender, who is seated at the table. The sender studies the picture or object, at the same time sitting quietly relaxed, having achieved this condition by means of the excercise previously described. In the meantime the recorder will write a description of this object or picture in the record book, in which he has already entered the other necessary data. Now, at the exact time he and the recorder at the receiver's end have previously determined, he gives the word to begin.

At once the sender concentrates upon the object or picture, examining it carefully, with a deliberate intention to transmit it to the receiver. In a quiet, relaxed way, he continues to look at it. *There must be no strain whatsoever*, whether physical or mental. At the same time, he should quietly assume in his mind that the receiver is actually in the room, quite close to him. The stronger this assumption becomes, the better for the success of the experiment. To assume the close proximity of the receiver has a very real effect, as the doubts and inhibitions about the projection of images over a distance will have been removed temporarily from the sender's subconscious.

The actual sending of the message should not take more than twenty to thirty seconds, and the sender should then cease his activity.

Procedure Used by Receiver

The procedure to used by the receiver is slightly different. He should be in the same relaxed condition as the sender. Now, for about five seconds, he deliberately reaches out to the sender, with the intention of receiving from him the message being held in his brain. Then the receiver should rest quietly and wait for any impressions that may come to him. These he should describe aloud, and here a small tape recorder is invaluable. If he wishes, he may at the same time write down the impressions, and make a drawing of any image he receives. He should also record any sound, scent, taste or tactile impressions he receives as a background to the main impression. To do all this will obviously take several minutes, and ten minutes to a quarter of an hour may be allowed. The impressions arrive in one block in the receiver's subconscious, but they take time to filter into his conscious mind, and for this reason time must be given. Some impressions may not come up until several hours later, and it is this delayed reception that frequently complicates these experiments.

The receiver should now rest from the mental attitude he had adopted and return to normal. He can take advantage of this mental rest period to move round the room to help break the mental train which the experiment has started in his mind. He will then be fresh for the next experiment. The recorder, in the meantime, has switched on the tape recorder at the start of the experiment, and has turned it off when the receiver has finished giving his impressions. Should a tape recorder not be used, then the recorder must write down whatever the receiver says in his report of the impressions he is receiving. This may not be so easy unless the recorder can use shorthand, and in every way it is best if a tape recorder can be obtained.

The recorder should enter a full account of all the

conditions which prevailed at the time of the experiment. It sometimes happens that some new condition comes up, and this must be recorded, as it may have a very important bearing upon the results obtained. The number of experiments to be tried at any one session is a matter of convenience and the wishes of all concerned. It should be kept in mind that tired, bored or unwilling senders and receivers are very unlikely to obtain any positive results. We suggest a minimum of five experiments in any one session for beginners in telepathy, but as proficiency grows, this could be extended. It is important to make certain that neither the sender nor the receiver should be allowed to leave their respective rooms until they have returned to normal consciousness.

Delayed Reception

We have referred to "delayed reception," and we may enlarge somewhat upon this phenomenon. The impressions are received in a block, as it were, and not all of them arrive in the receiver's conscious mind at the same time. Later on, some of these delayed impressions will emerge under some new conditions. So the receiver should note down any irrelevant thought images which suddenly pop up from nowhere, and because of the tendency for these impressions to fade quickly, it is helpful if he writes them down as they appear.

This description of a typical experiment in telepathic transmission is intended to form the outline of any such experiments on your part, and has been compiled from my experiences over many years.

10

Hypnotic and Mesmeric Telepathy

IN the last chapter we considered the usual technique of telepathic training. There are, however, other ways in which the faculty may be brought into action. One of these is the use of mesmerism or hypnotism. I make a differentiation between these two, although they are usually regarded as the same thing under different names. From a good deal of practical experience, I am of the opinion that "hypnotism" is only past of a much larger subject.

The name hypnotism was coined by Dr. James Braid. He had been at some exhibitions of mesmerism, and had been struck by certain things that could not be attributed to fraud. At that time, the subject of mesmerism was being hotly discussed in medical circles, and many charlatans had found mesmerism a very lucrative field. The actual phenomena were named after their discoverer, Dr. Anton Mesmer. For various reasons, he fell afoul of the French medical establishment of his day, and two commissions were appointed to examine the alleged phenomena of "animal magnetism." The commission of 1784 was most unfavorable to the claims of the mesmerists, but the second, in 1831, was favorable. However, the implacable hostility of the medical establishment in both Britain and France was such that able doctors, like Esdaile in India (who performed major amputations at a special mesmeric hospital which the Indian government helped him to run), and Dr. Elliotson in London (who was hounded out of his hospital post by his fellow doctors), were subjected to floods of abuse and vituperation from their medical colleagues.

In connection with the work done by Esdaile in India, it is on record that he performed such major surgical work as the amputation of limbs and the removal of huge scrotal tumors without the use of any anaesthetic. Anyone who has read the history of surgery before the discovery of general anaesthetics, chloroform and ether will have gained some idea of the terrible suffering involved in surgery at that time. The great virtues of the use of the mesmeric trance state were that the patient felt no pain, and the post-operative shock—from which the majority of patients who had been operated on usually died—was reduced to a minimum. Despite this fact of painless surgery, one eminent medical authority publicly proclaimed that Esdaile's patients, when suffering a major amputation of, say a leg or arm, were really conscious, but pretending they didn't feel anything! Or else that they were in a faint! Esdaile's reply to this bit of foolishness was to invite the eminent authority to undergo such an operation after being persuaded to faint. Needless to say, the challenge was declined.

Animal Magnetism

The whole teaching of the mesmerists was that a certain vital energy which they called "animal magnetism" was capable of being sent from the operator's body, and when directed upon anyone willing to receive it, produced certain abnormal conditions in that person. Due to the climate of medical science at that time, and unfortunately for a very long time after, the possibility of nervous energy being transferred from one person to another was unthinkable and scientifically blasphemous. It just couldn't happen, so those who said it could were liars, charlatans or self-deceived.

However such claims continued to be made, causing a good deal of annoyance to the faithful in medical circles. Then Dr. Braid put forward a new idea, based upon his observations of some "mesmeric" exhibitions he had witnessed. These shows, at music halls and other places, did much to degrade the whole subject, although both mesmeric and hypnotic public shows of this kind were not put under any restrictions until quite recently. Dr. Braid's theory enabled the medical profession to accept some of the mesmeric claims, and yet oppose the main theories of the mesmerists. Particularly was this the case with the alleged transference of energy from one person to another, for Braid showed that it was possible to induce certain abnormal states of mind and body simply by the use of verbal suggestion, this suggestion becoming particularly powerful through the use of "hypnotic" techniques which he had evolved himself.

So a remnant of the old mesmeric technique remained, but those of us who have used both methods are firmly convinced that it is much harder to work as a mesmerist than as a hypnotist. The new parapsychological work now being carried out in Russia and the Iron Curtain countries, as well as in America, seems to be justifying Mesmer to an increasing degree. The "Kirlian photography" which clearly shows some form of energy leaving the body is but one piece of the accumulating proof for mesmeric theories.

Higher Psychic Phenomena

It is true that many of the mesmeric phenomena can be produced by hypnotic methods which, like those of mesmerism, gain control over the subconscious level of the subject's mind. At the same time, many of the higher psychic phenomena which are obtainable by mesmeric methods are rarely produced by purely hypnotic techniques. When hypnotism does produce the higher phenomena, it is an observed fact that the hypnotist con-

97

cerned usually has the characteristic physique of a mesmerist, so it may be that it was the unconscious possession of the mesmeric power that contributed to his success. It is not safe to make generalizations, and there are probably many unknown factors concerned here.

To conclude this part of our treatment of the mesmeric and hypnotic techniques, we may also say that quite apart from the action of the operator, the subject can be trained to induce the trance state without any outside aid. This is known as "auto-hypnotism" or "auto-mesmerism," and indeed some schools of hypnotism hold that all hypnotic phenomena are self-induced by the subject, led by suggestion along a certain line of thought.

Trance State

In the induction of telepathy by the use of hypnotism or mesmerism, suggestion is largely used; the subject is told to mentally visit a distant place and describe what he sees there. Then he is given a definite body of suggestions, which are designed to make him realize his own inner power. All this time he is becoming closely linked with the operator by a curious line of rapport or sympathy, and it becomes possible for the operator to induce the trance state in him at a distance, when he has no knowledge that the experiment is being tried. Some of the Russian experimenters report considerable success along this line. Here of course we have a definite telepathic link between the subject and the operator, though the result is a one-way communication. The great advantage of the psychic rapport established between the operator and his subject is that it rapidly stimulates the telepathic faculty into action, and, indeed, it is one of the most effective methods of doing this.

The disadvantage is that it is apt to produce a curious psychological dependence of the subject upon his operator, which can cause considerable trouble. Because of this I would not advise anyone, unless they have a good practical knowledge of mesmerism or hypnotism, to attempt the use of either for the induction of telepathy.

In passing I may say that the "developing circles" technique used in the spiritualist movement for the development of the psychic faculties is an example of the combined use of both the hypnotic and mesmeric methods. A "pool" of psychic energy is formed by several people sitting together with the general idea of developing psychic powers. The dominant ideas of the group will affect whatever results are obtained. Here the psychic energy directed upon the members by the pool of energy donated by them all, is conditioned by the suggestive power of the dominant idea, and this causes the psychic faculties to begin to manifest themselves. Whether, as the spiritualist would claim, telepathic impulses and energies derived from other beings are also present, is a question outside the scope of this book.

Hallucinogens

Another way of developing telepathic sensitivity is by the use of the drugs. Some of the "hallucinogens" have been used for this purpose in all cultures and in all ages. In recent years there has been a revival of these drugs. In some cases they certainly do arouse the psychic faculties, but in an unregulated and chaotic way, and with the accompaniment of undesirable physical side effects. For this reason I would advise anyone who may be tempted to use these drugs in order to awaken the telepathic faculty to leave them severely alone. I have had many come to me who regretted having used them for this purpose, and who wanted to get rid of the unpleasant symptoms which they were experiencing. "Easy is the descent to hell," says the old adage, and I would add, "difficult, exceedingly difficult, is the way back."

Some people say that the manner in which psychic impressions reach the brain cells is by an organo-chemical process, in which certain substances are secreted by the body glands in infinitesimal doses. If this is the case, if drugs of any kind are to be used to arouse the telepathic faculty, it might be better to take them in the exceedingly minute doses prescribed by the homeopaths, one drop to a million or so parts of water, rather than in the crude doses which the foolish drug addict consumes. However, the best way is to leave drugs severely alone. The game isn't worth the candle.

Telepathy in Dreams

We now come to another way in which the telepathic images may be received, and this is through the imagery of dreams. There has been much research work undertaken on the occurrence of telepathy in dreams. The same procedure used in waking telepathy may be used in experiments with dream telepathy but it must obviously be modified to suit the slightly altered conditions. The sender need not alter his method, but the receiver must change his somewhat. He has to realize that any impressions he may bring through from the sleep state will have penetrated the dream layers of his subconscious, and will be affected by their passage through that part of his mind. Modern psychology has given us a picture of some of the workings of these dream layers, and this suggests that among other things, there are hosts of mental images strongly charged with emotion always trying to rise from the subconscious into the waking consciousness, but which are continually being thrust back by a kind of mental barrier. Only by disguising themselves in some way can they get through into the waking mind. The disguise they use is symbolism, and the dream images are the symbols of the motive power behind the suppressed thoughts.

There is, therefore, a true science of dream interpretation. This was first brought into prominence by the work of Freud and his pupil Jung. To Freud, sex was the chief energy in all dream images. Since his idea of sex was more liberal than that of his contemporaries, the popular mind seized upon his theories, as they seemed to get away from the narrow, restricted ideas of the Victorian era. Jung gave an even wider interpretation of sex than did Freud. It is to be noted that Freud, whom many materialistic psychologists seem to regard as their patron saint, wrote a treatise upon the faculty of telepathy.

11

Telepathy and Super-physical Healing

WHEN the psychologists began to use the methods of dream analysis, they found that in addition to the flood of images that welled up from the depths of the mind, there were images and impressions that did not seem to have any connection with the others. Although the psychologists tried their best to fit them in, these odd thoughts and impressions just would not be accommodated in the ordinary dream picture. In many cases, these stray images were found to be derived from the thinking of people who were either in the vicinity or were in some way sympathetically linked with the dreamer.

Following up this clue, definite experiments were made with one person sending some image or picture or message to the sleeping receiver. There was positive evidence that such telepathic messages and ideas were picked up by the sleeping subject, and appeared in the dream images that were remembered when returning to the waking state. But if we are thus affected by the influence of one mind upon us when we are in the sleeping state, then it is equally possible for us to be continually receiving such images from the collective mind of all around us. Here there is a curious indirect link between these experiments and the results obtained by the late Edgar Cayce. Apparently he could and did link up with people whom he had never seen physically, and of whom he knew nothing.

Experiments with Plants

May it not be, as some mystics assert, that we are always linked in mind and spirit with all humanity—indeed with all living things? There are some recent experiments with plants that seem to show that they are affected by the thoughts of those around them. In some experiments the mental image in the operator's mind that he was going to burn the leaf on a plant resulted in a definite reaction being recorded by an instrument attached to the plant, which registered the sap and other pressures in the plant. The nature mystic proclaiming the unity of all nature seems to have anticipated this discovery.

The occultists have long proclaimed the existence of what they term the "astral light," described as a realm of thought and emotion surrounding the entire planet, and extending beyond the confines of the system. All life lives and moves in this enveloping atmosphere and the astral serves as a means of communication and contact between all forms of life on earth. Even the so-called dead energies of the mineral kingdom are swept up into this great unity of all life. Therefore it is also claimed by the occultists that this region of the astral light is a place in which great super-physical energies are to be found, and it is alleged that these energies affect all life upon this planet.

Thus we have a reservoir of super-physical power which, it is said, can be tapped by the use of certain methods that have been elaborated through the centuries. Indeed, it may often happen that quite without any conscious knowledge of the occult techniques, some people do make contact with one or other of these forces and use them in a hit or miss fashion. Some of these energies are lumped together under the general name of healing power, and there are many associations of people who try to use them in the healing of the sick. Healing is such a very complex subject, with so many emotional overtones, that it needs very careful handling, and if we refer to it here, it is mainly because we believe, from our own experience, that the element of telepathy is present in most super-physical healing.

Transferred Energy

In a paper read to a parapsychological conference, a doctor put forward a theory—based on careful experimental work which she had undertaken—which suggested that certain forms of super-physical healing were due to energy being transferred from the healer to the patient, and that this energy used the telepathic impulse as a kind of carrier wave. "Absent healing," practiced by many healers, may well be due to the body's inherent healing power which receives this energy and uses it to good effect.

Many healers, however, insist that the power is directed and strengthened by beings of a super-physical order and others believe that the power comes from, and is directed by, God. In the sense that *all* power comes from God, both schools of thought are probably right, but each school claims that it has the truth, and that the other is deceived. There are, of course, those who are of the opinion that *both* schools are right in much that they claim for their methods of healing. At the same time it is possible that the healing energies may not, in every case, be carried on the telepathic wave, but become effective in a different way.

We have referred to the healing power in the body; this inner energy, which is always trying to keep the body in health, may be aroused to vigorous action and produce results within the body that are regarded as miracles of healing. It could well be that it is the stimulus given to that inner power by the telepathic impulse which really heals. Here again, however, we can surely regard that wonderful organizing healing principle within our organism as a manifestation of the Divine Will which energizes and directs all manifestation. Possibly the aroused inner power also presses into its service many of the forces and energies of the astral light.

Super-physical Beings

I have said that some healers maintain they are helped by super-physical beings, and others have also said that they work in close cooperation with those beings, who are usually alleged to be discarnate people. Sensitive persons helped by these healers have sometimes perceived the form of the healer standing beside them, even when they were unaware of the time when he would be sending out the "absent healing." It would seem that some energy-charged telepathic impulse was perceived by the sensitive person in the form of the person sending it. There are many cases of such "phantasms of the living" recorded in the annals of the S.P.R., but we should remember that there is a good deal of evidence for what is termed "astral projection," in which the consciousness of the person apparently leaves the physical body in what appears to be a finer body—usually known as the "astral body." So it might be that the healer, in his astral body, was actually in the vicinity of the patient.

Some patients for whom absent healing was being done by a healer have seen psychically the forms of those discarnate spirits who, it was claimed, were the unseen helpers of that particular healer. There is no reason, in my opinion, why one method should be thought to be the only legitimate method of super-normal healing, but the subject can arouse such emotional reactions that I cannot go into it further here. I have simply tried to show how telepathy may be one of the root principles in these forms of healing.

12

Telepathic Thought-forms

THERE are very many men and women who are content to use the telepathic faculty without worrying about any theories as to its nature. It is sufficient for them that the faculty works, though others want to know *how*. These people have before them a very wide field of research. For instance, there is the question of "thought-forms," where definite forms are built up on the inner levels by the power of thought, in the same way as in ordinary telepathic work, but these forms may persist as a kind of separate object, attached to people or objects.

As an illustration of this, I was present when a psychic sensitive was describing various appearances which she saw around people in the audience. Coming to one lady, she described in great detail a most unusual looking person, and asked her if she recognized this person. "Oh yes, I do recognize him," she said, "he is the principal character in a novel I am writing, and I've given up quite a lot of time to build up his appearance in my mind." Here was definite psychic reception of a carefully built up thought-form, and emphasizes the fact that the psychic faculties are really modifications of a basic psychic sense, in the same way that the ordinary physical senses are also modifications of the one basic physical sense of "touch." In the case of the psychic faculties this basic sense is the psychic equivalent of touch, and is what we have been studying as "telepathy."

We have just said that thought-forms can be attached to objects and people. That objects are affected by being linked with certain thought-forms is the principle behind the "blessing" of objects which is a part of all the great ceremonial religions. These forms are charged with energies of one kind or another, and tend to induce in any person who wears the object or comes into contact with it, emotions similar to those with which the thought-form was charged. In the case of consecration such forms are linked with certain Beings who are held to be able, through this link, to permanently use such objects as channels through which they can affect the personality of anyone who makes contact with them.

Poltergeist Phenomena

There is another way in which thought can affect physical objects. Under certain conditions of mental strain it seems that some partial deflection of the inner energies of an individual can take place. This seems to occur in many cases in young people during puberty. Some subconscious telepathic impulse seems to go out from them charged with inner energies and this may actually cause physical manifestations, such as the movement of small objects, luminous appearances, noises, and so on. Such manifestations are usually known as "poltergeist phenomena," and they can be a very real annoyance to those who have to live where they occur. They can be dealt with by helping the boy or girl who is the focus from which they emanate.

I have investigated several of these cases, and as a general rule—after the person concerned was given psychological assistance—the disturbances ceased. In a few cases, however, it appeared that there were other factors in the case, such as the conscious or unconscious telepathic action from super-physical beings. A proportion of these seemed to be discarnate spirits of the dead, but some were apparently non-human beings who had become entangled in the aura of the victim. Usually, where human spirits appeared to be concerned, I found that a quietly reasoned approach to them, together with a sincere desire to help them out of their present condition, was sufficient to break the telepathic web in which they had become entangled.

Exorcism

With the other entities it was necessary to use some form of exorcism. This whole question of super-physical interference is one in which it is literally true that fools rush in where angels fear to tread. We see this now in the increasing number of priests of the Anglican Church, and ministers of some of the Protestant denominations, who are launching out as "exorcists." They appear to make somewhat sweeping claims of success for their activities, but how far those claims are justified is doubtful.

Curiously enough, two or three centuries ago, the Anglican Church had a similar rash of clerical exorcists, who competed against each other openly, until the Anglican bishops stopped them. In the Roman Church such exorcism was only allowed by permission of the bishop. That clerical exorcism can be of avail is undeniable, but some of the antics of would-be exorcists are a source of scandal to the Church.

The spiritualists have methods of their own to clear such psychic conditions, and they are at least as effective as those of the clergy. Where it is possible for members of the two camps to work together, results are very good, and under the auspices of the Churches' Fellowship for Psychical and Spiritual Studies, this is being done. Both sides learn from one another in the Fellowship.

General Summary

We have studied the subject of telepathy in a discursive way, for it is so great and has so many overtones that it is possible only to give some hints that the earnest researcher can follow up. Perhaps it may be well to make a general summary of the possibilities and indicate what lines of research can be fruitful.

We are all, to some extent, rather shortsighted in our approach to these matters. We think of ourselves as personally distinct and separate, but this separateness is an illusion. Behind the mask of the personality our true self is to be found, and that true self is not limited to the three-dimensional universe, the only one of which the material self is aware. Through the various powers now beginning to show themselves in many persons, we are gaining some insight into our real nature, and finding that the separate self is in itself an illusion, built through the ages of evolution so that we can work and express ourselves in the material world. However, behind the mask of the personality, is the real self, and this lives and moves in accordance with the greater cosmic laws, and in dimensions of existence of which the personal self knows very little. Only at times does something of this true self emerge in the personal consciousness, and under conditions of which we have only a partial knowledge.

Thought, as we conceive it, is but a shadow of true Thought, but nevertheless it does link us with that true Thought, and in our telepathic practice it is possible for us to occasionally make some form of contact with this higher realm. Then for a short time the limitations of the lower self are to some extent lifted and we begin to know ourselves even as we are known in that larger life. There, in that realm of Light, we see and realize that we are never really separate from anyone else—we are all linked together in the One Life—and there we find the justification for all human schemes which seek to bring into manifestation the Brotherhood of Man on earth. Our earthly concepts of that brotherhood are partial of necessity, but they are reflections of the true brotherhood which has not to be made, but only to be *realized*.

Our telepathic research may bring us into realization of brotherhood for a fleeting minute only, but the results of this flash of true consciousness can mold and direct our lives from that moment onward.

Telepathy may start as an interesting game, be continued as a worthwhile piece of research, and lead to a realization of our part in the greater Life of which we are a part; thus we have the chance to do the Will of the Eternal. And in the doing of that Will, we shall, as the blessed souls told Dante, find our true Peace.

PART III

Psychometry

13

A Tale to Unfold

YOU must often have heard people say, when looking at some object of historical interest, "What a tale it could tell, if it could only speak." Those of us who have practical knowledge of what is popularly known as ESP know from our own experience that this saying is true. The historic article, indeed every article, not only has a tale to tell, but it is telling it constantly, in the same way, to use an analogy, that the magnetic tape of a tape-recorder has imprinted upon it words or music which, under suitable conditions, may be heard again and again as they are reproduced by the machine.

It is true that there is no instrument, electrical or otherwise, that can reproduce for us the sights and sounds, the emotions, passions and thoughts that have been recorded upon material objects. Certain people, however, appear to have a kind of "sixth sense" that enables them to pick up these hidden vibrations and impressions, and bring them into their waking consciousness. Such people are called "psychometrists."

The word is derived from two Greek words, *psyche*, meaning "the soul," and *metron*, signifying a "measure." By this definition, psychometry is the power to measure and interpret "the soul of things."

This name was given to the faculty by Professor Denton, whose experiments with his sister's sensitivity to geological specimens are described in Part I. You will recall that he found that if she held a geological specimen to her forehead, even though it was carefully wrapped up so that its nature could not be guessed at through its appearance she was able to obtain through vivid pictures which arose in her mind's eye, some knowledge of the past history of the particular specimen being tested.

A Psychometrist at Work

Let us now watch, in imagination, a psychometrist at work. There are so-called psychometry meetings, where a professional psychometrist deals with a number of articles brought by members of the audience. As a rule, the objects are placed in separate compartments on a tray, in order, it is said, to prevent the influences of one article affecting others near it. This, as we know from practical experience, is not always a complete safeguard against mixed influences. In this connection, a story from the beginnings of modern psychometric experimentation may be of interest. A certain lady who had been told of this strange new power, had gone to bed one night, and was lying awake thinking about psychometry as it had been described to her. Suddenly she determined to make a practical test to see if there was anything in the idea. So, getting out of bed in the dark she went downstairs without a light and from her writing desk chose at random a letter from a collection of letters which she kept in chronological order in one of the desk drawers. She duly held the letter to her forehead and tried to "see" something about the person who had written it, and was rewarded by finding a flood of impressions coming to her mind. These impressions built up the character and general outlook of one man, a very strong-willed and powerful person. Full of excitement at this proof of the reality of this strange power, she went back to bed without even attempting to see if her impressions were correct, she felt so sure that they were.

Waking in the morning, she remembered her midnight psychometric experiment, and eagerly looked at the letter, which she had brought up with her and now lay on the table beside her bed. To her great astonishment and disillusionment, the character of the writer of the letter in no way whatsoever resembled that which she had felt in her experiment. Full of gloom she went down to replace the letter in its correct position in the drawer. As she did so, she glanced at the letter which lay next to it in the bundle, and saw with delight that all she had had felt when attempting to psychometrize the letter she had chosen was to be found in the character of the writer of the one lying next to it. The strong virile character had impressed itself not only on the actual letter, but also upon the weak influence of the letter next to it.

An Imaginary Reading

Returning to our psychometric readings, we see that the psychometrist takes an article and either holds it in his hand or presses it to his forehead, and proceeds to describe that which he feels and "sees" as he comes into psychic contact with it. Here is an imaginary reading, based upon our own experience with a good psychometrist:

"I see before me a wide expanse of water—I think it is the sea. Yes, I feel it is the Atlantic ocean. I am standing on the deck of a ship—it seems to be a wooden ship—it is a warship of some kind, for I see guns—muzzle-loading guns of Nelson's time or thereabouts. The sea appears to be a deep blue and is very calm, and the sunlight is strong. In the distance there is a low coastline, and I see, nestling in the low hills that rise behind the sand dunes of the coast, a town of white-walled buildings. My attention is drawn to a man who is evidently the captain of this ship. He is dressed in the uniform of an officer in the Royal Navy of Nelson's time. I feel that some of the trees on the hills are olive trees, and I think this must be either Spain or Portugal. The ship appears to be taking part in blockading this seaport town.

"Now I am looking at a ring—a gold ring with a large amethyst set in it—it is this same ring which I am now holding—I feel a sense of power and authority in connection with this. Why, it belongs to this officer, but it takes me back very many years before this time. I seem to be in Italy—at least that is the impression I get—and I feel that the original owner of this ring lived in Italy and was a prominent Churchman of his time—I sense he was a bishop or some such dignitary—there is a sound as of Latin being chanted, and I feel that this ring goes back to the time of the Renaissance.

"This must have been handed down to the captain as an heirloom and has in the same way been passed down to its present possessor.

"Now I want to come to the person who gave in this ring for a reading. You are at present at the parting of the ways, and you are finding it very difficult indeed to decide which path to choose—they seem equally compeling. I feel, however, that within a short time—and this will be measured in days, not weeks, the matter will become clear to you and the way forward be opened up. Do not make any sudden move until this clear indication of the correct line to take presents itself."

The recipient of this message confirms that the ring did in fact belong to one of Nelson's sea captains, an ancestor of his, and it was at one time owned by one of the great Catholic bishops of the Renaissance. He also agrees that he is indeed approaching a crisis in his material affairs, and cannot make up his mind as to which will be the correct course to follow.

This is a typical psychometric reading of the better type. Some such readings are much better, some very much worse, but this gives a fair idea of what may be expected.

You will notice that there are three definite levels in this particular reading. There is the description of the original owner of the ring and his general surroundings, there is the description of the sea captain and his general conditions, and finally there is a statement made concerning the present owner of the article. The first level we may term its primary record, the second its secondary level, the level concerning the present and future conditions of the owner of the ring as the tertiary level. These three levels will be found, in varying proportions, in all psychometric readings.

The Source of Knowledge

The question arises, how has the psychometrist obtained his knowledge? In the majority of cases we can rule out collusion between the psychometrist and the owner of the article concerned. Where such collusion does happen, it is soon detected and dealt with. We are left with a very considerable body of statements which have to be explained in some other way. A detached study of the matter usually reveals the presence of much that is not in any way evidential. It is due to the psychological fact that the level of acceptance, if we may so call it, varies considerably from one person to another. There are those whose critical faculty is slight, and such people will accept as evidence much that more critical people would not regard as being in any way evidential. So what we may term the credibility factor has to be taken into account when judging the statements made. We would point out, however, that often what appears to be a triviality may have a real significance for the person concerned, and it is sometimes these very trivialities that provide conclusive proof of the accuracy of the statements made by the psychometrist.

When, however, we have discounted those vague general statements which are obviously non-evidential, but are what we might describe as verbal padding, we are left with positive and detailed statements that are truly evidential, and that cannot be explained away by any theories of fraud or wishful thinking. So we are back to our question of how these evidential statements came into the mind of the psychometrist. It was obviously not through the ordinary five senses. One answer, of course, is that the knowledge was received telepathically from the mind of the owner of the article which was being psychometrized. This may be so in some instances, but we feel that by invoking the telepathic explanation, we are simply substituting one form of extrasensory perception for another, and in many cases the information simply does not exist within the mind of any living person. The skeptic is therefore often driven to formulating a "pool of knowledge," a "cosmic memory," from which, it is alleged, the psychometrist draws his information. It is an attractive theory, and, despite the way in which it is sometimes employed against the claims of the spiritualists, it does fit in with the results of psychometrical practice. It will be useful, perhaps, to take a look at this idea of a pool of knowledge upon which we may draw under certain conditions.

Those who are acquainted with the work of the late Dr. C. G. Jung will remember that he put forward in his writings the idea of what he called the Collective Unconscious, which lies behind the normal individual consciousness with which we are all familiar. Each person, in the depths of his subconscious nature, is linked up directly with this collective unconscious. Because of this we may, under certain circumstances, bring into the waking consciousness some of the knowledge which lies in those hidden realms of the mind.

The Astral Light

This concept of the collective unconscious is familiar to anyone who has studied the teachings of what is usually called occultism. By them the collective unconscious is known as the astral light and it is held that the activities of this collective unconscious work through many varying degrees of an immaterial "substance" which underlies all physical matter. It is further held that this underlying substance not only contains the memory records, both conscious and subconscious, of all life upon the physical planet, but it is also the channel through which the all-embracing Consciousness of the Creator and Sustainer of this universe holds all manifestation, on all levels of existence, within Its power and control.

In the East, the divine life and consciousness is said to work in and through what is known as "Akasha," and for this reason we find the term "the Akashic Records" employed to refer to this cosmic memory. This is, of course, only a very rough outline of a very intricate system of philosophy.

It is further taught that these Akashic Records are reflected at varying levels in the astral light, and are liable to suffer some distortion when near the emotional and mental currents which surge through the collective unconscious of the planet. So we have the concept of an all-embracing mind and consciousness not far removed from earth-life and its struggles, but actually immanent within it as well as remaining in its fullness above and beyond all manifestation. It is also held that by virtue of his own innate divinity, man may become, in varying degree, en rapport with that divine consciousness, and in proportion as he does this, he is able to make contact with that cosmic memory, of which his own personal memory is but a fractional part.

With James and Fechner and many other philosophers, the occultists also hold that this planet is not a mere inert ball of mineral matter swinging through the heavens, but is the body or vehicle of a mighty but simple life, and because of this it possesses its own memory of all that has happened upon it. Every particle of matter is, by this hypothesis, understood to be a means whereby the Anima Mundi, the Soul of the World, may be contacted.

The Reflecting Ether

So we come to the simple definition of Denton and his co-workers, that in psychometry we are making contact with and reading in the indelible memory of the soul of things. Incidentally, the occultists say that this planetary memory is recorded in what they term the "reflecting ether" of the planet. This reflecting ether not only holds the planetary memory, but also reflects the foreknowledge of the Divine Mind which is ever in the true Akashic Records. Thus, through the reflecting ether, some glimpses of futurity, some "shadows cast before" may be obtained by the psychometrist, but such foretelling of the future will depend for its accuracy upon how clearly those reflections of the Divine Mind are being mirrored in the depths of the memory of the *Anima Mundi*.

Having given you something of the theories and hypotheses which have been put forward to explain the phenomena of psychometry, it is as well if we get down to earth and concentrate upon developing the faculty; one can always argue about the metaphysics of it at a later date when personal practical experience has been gained.

It is not necessary that you should hold any particular theory about psychometry; you can just develop the faculty and use it without accepting any one theory, just as one can see without any expert knowledge of optics. Once you have developed the psychometric faculty you can use it, as indeed you can use all faculties, both physical and superphysical, for whatever purpose appeals to you. Remember, however, that increased ability brings with it increased responsibility to use it in the right way, and here, of course, you come up against the moral aspect of such development. See Chapter Two for a discussion on this aspect.

14

Concerning Psychic Gifts

AN idea has grown up that psychic faculties, such as clairvoyance, clairaudience, psychometry and so on, are peculiar gifts bestowed by nature on certain individuals, and are not faculties possessed by all mankind. This belief has three aspects. First of all, there is the old pagan idea of the gods showering gifts upon men. More particularly, since it was thought that such psychic qualities enabled some kind of link to be made between the gods and their worshippers, the psychic qualities, above all others, were regarded in a special way, and around their use there gathered the numinous atmosphere of religion.

At the heart of the primitive religions of mankind was to be found the idea of the oracle, the seer, the soothsayer, and behind the official exoteric religion of the day an inner or esoteric teaching and practice.

When Christianity began to emerge as a religion there arose various groups which are generally listed together as Gnostics, for they claimed to have direct personal knowledge of spiritual things. Many of those who had turned to Christianity from one or another of the old Mystery Faiths, felt that a great deal of their previous knowledge could be "baptized into Christ" and many of them became influential teachers in the infant Church.

Psychic Faculties

It is worth noting that in both the classical mysteries and early Christian Gnosticism, the use of the psychic faculties did not imply any such communications with the spirits of discarnate human beings as modern spiritualism envisages, but was concerned with contact with spiritual beings of various kinds. When, by any mischance, what appeared to be a discarnate human being made itself felt, it was held that something had gone wrong, and steps were taken to prevent its recurrence. It is worth emphasizing the point that, neither Egyptian "Kerheb," Elusinean Hierophant, Neo-Platonic Theurgist nor Christian Gnostic sought communication with the "dead" through mediumship, though all forms of psychic faculty were known to them. This, of course, does not disprove the spiritualistic explanation, but as many spiritualists have claimed that such contact *must* have been made, and that only with human spirits, it is necessary to point out that although the possibility of contact with the dead cannot be ruled out, those whom we have mentioned did not in any way regard it as the primary object of their psychic practices.

In a well-known passage in one of his letters to his Corinthian converts, St. Paul gives instructions to the small groups of Christians who met together for spiritual communion and prayer. It must be kept in mind that the early "Followers of the Way," as the Christians were first called, took the promise of their Lord and Master very seriously indeed. He had told them that He would send the Holy Spirit to them, to lead them, and they believed that the influence of this same Holy Spirit was to be found in all the gatherings of the faithful. It was, they said, a "Spirit-filled Church."

In the small groups gathered together for worship and communion, psychic phenomena manifested, just as they did many centuries later in the similar groups of the Society of Friends (more commonly known as the Quakers.)

122

Here again, in the Quaker Meetings it is held to be the power and presence of the Spirit, rather than the efforts of the so-called dead, which produces them.

Paul indeed says that the one and selfsame Spirit apportions to each person a particular "gift" or "charism," and here we find a link with the pagan and also the Jewish idea of the gods or God, giving gifts to men. An unfortunate translation of the Greek has made Paul refer to *spiritual* gifts, but the praise is more correctly translated as 'psychic' gifts, i.e., pertaining to the soul or "psyche," rather than to the spirit; to Paul, man was a trinity of body, soul and spirit.

So, from pagan antiquity, through the Christian ages up to the present time, these psychic faculties have been regarded as gifts from above, and this attitude of mind has also been applied to all the faculties of man. Thus, we speak of a gifted speaker, a gifted artist or a gifted musician. In all these cases we are using the thought forms of the past, and this is especially noticeable when we come to deal with the psychic faculties.

There is, however, another point of view, which is implicit in the teachings which form the basis of the philosophy of life of the present writer. This is that the psychic faculties are present in all men and in a latent fashion in all life, but in some cases they are working above the threshold of the normal waking consciousness, whereas in the majority they are below that threshold. How far they lie below that threshold determines whether it is worth the effort needed to bring them into conscious working activity. In some cases they seem to spring spontaneously into activity. In others, years of "sitting for development" will fail to bring them into action. Most people, however, lie between these two extremes. They can develop or unfold such faculties, but the time needed to do this varies with each individual.

However, to unfold a faculty is one thing; to stabilize it and have it under one's control is quite another! It is here that so many would-be psychics fail the test. They make no attempt to discipline and train their psychic ability, and this very often springs from the mistaken idea of "gifts," already considered. We shall return to this whole question of stabilization, discipline and training later on in this book, but we felt we should just refer to it at this point.

We come now to the ethical point of view. As we have already pointed out, an unfortunate translation has connected these faculties with the idea of "spirituality." It is therefore worthwhile to consider what this term means, and how far it may be applied to these super-normal faculties which lie within each of us. In the early Christian Church, there arose a curious "heresy" or point of view (for that is what the word heresy originally meant) which made a clear-cut division or "dichotomy" between "spirit" and "matter."

Spirit and Matter

The beginning of this came into prominence in the teachings of a certain Manes, a Christian teacher who had adopted some of the ideas of the Persian religion of Zoroastrianism. Spirit and matter were regarded as eternally opposed and matter was held to be absolutely evil. This heresy, though condemned by the great Councils of the Church, has never been entirely banished from Christendom, and has appeared in various guises again and again. It was the basis of the Puritan streak which runs through the whole of Christian history, and it caused any natural and necessary reaction to licentious teaching and conduct to become badly emphasized and out of balance, resulting in a teaching and practice equally detrimental to the true development of the spirit of man.

Although those schools of thought that teach the use of the psychic faculty claim to have become free from orthodox ideas, they are still apparently bound by this faulty translation of the New Testament concerning psychic gifts, and very many of their followers persist in regarding these faculties as *spiritual* gifts.

Insofar as all man's powers and faculties are spiritual, in the true sense, for matter is but one manifestation of spirit, they are correct, *but* and this is a big "but," if they regard *psychic* faculties as spiritual, then they must also so regard man's physical faculties as equally spiritual, otherwise they fall into the Manichaean heresy.

Unfortunately, however, the error persists that the possession of a psychic faculty of necessity means that the person concerned is also a "spiritual" person in the ethical and moral sense. Anyone who is acquainted at first hand with the world of psychism and allied subjects knows full well that this is not the case, yet the idea is strongly entrenched, and will no doubt be with us for a long time. As we have seen, it has a long history, and cannot be eliminated in five minutes.

The fact remains that the possessor of psychic faculties and mediumistic abilities is not necessarily a person of high moral and spiritual character. Indeed, the reverse is very often the case.

Telepathic Suggestions

We have already referred to the varying depths of the mind in which these psychic faculties may be latent. Let us now consider the case of one in whom these faculties are very near the surface of the subconscious, but are not within the conscious field of the waking self. They are, however, constantly acting in the subconscious level, receiving impressions from the thoughts and emotions of others around them. All these impressions are coming into their minds as suggestions, some good, and some bad, and are constantly altering the whole consciousness. All men are linked together in this manner, and, quite apart from our common subconscious base in what is known as the collective unconscious of the race, we are ever surrounded by and immersed in a swirling sea of thought and emotion, through which flow rhythmic tides of energy to which we are ever responding, whether or not we are aware of it.

So it often happens that a woman adopts the life of a prostitute not because she consciously chose such a path, but because of the effect upon her partially awakened psychic senses of the thoughts and emotions of others concerning her. Her very sensitivity has betrayed her. If she was brought up with certain ideals of conduct in sexual matters, she may have resisted the combined pull of her natural instincts and the insidious suggestions that reached her through her hidden sensitivity. Then a time may have come when she was, for the moment, off guard, and the instinctive urges and the telepathic suggestions combined to lose her emotional and ethical balance, and so she fell into sin. But the blame for that fall may well lie with someone who, with virtuous respectability pre-judged her, and, by the weight of this thought (itself very often the product of thwarted sexual urges) contributed to her downfall. "Condemn not, that ye be not con-demned" is a very sound injunction.

A Code of Living

Because of this psychic interaction between ourselves and all around us, it is highly desirable that, if we would most truly be ourselves, we should consciously and de-liberately construct for our daily life and work a code of living, a standard of ethics and morals, which will pre-vent us from being at the mercy of these unseen but powerful influences in our environment. We know the necessity of such codes of thought and conduct in the face of the visible and tangible temptations we meet in ordinary waking life. Even more so are such codes needed as a guard against these unseen and intangible subcon-scious temptations.

Having established such a code of living, we may safely attempt to bring into the conscious waking mind the impressions which are being received by way of these submerged psychic senses. When thus brought under our conscious control, they cease to be the hidden uncharted sources of some of our irresponsible thinking, and we begin to be less affected by the composite "mob-mind" of those around. We are obeying the rule which in ancient days was inscribed over the Temple of the Mysteries: "Know Thyself!" When the psychic impressions are thus brought into consciousness, it is possible to judge their value and to deal with them within the code of living developed.

The reader is in a position to make use of them for his own true advancement in character, and, by being consciously aware of them he will no longer be at their mercy. He can observe the conditions which will allow them to work, and can also begin to assess their value to him in his life.

It is true that in the present state of our modern knowledge regarding these faculties, their exercise partakes far more fully of art, than science, but as progress is made in understanding the laws that govern their manifestation, it will be seen what a sublime science lies behind the workings of these super-normal faculties.

This science has never been entirely lost to mankind, though in the West it has apparently been obscured because of the type of civilization which has been built up here. In the East, however, it has persisted more openly in the various Yoga systems, fragments of which are being so assiduously peddled in the West at the present time. Much of this is a travesty of the true teaching. In both the East and West, however, there are those who are the initiates and custodians of this ageless wisdom, and they stand ready to assist those in the Western world who, at this momentous point in the history of man, are engaged in research work in this field of the super-normal.

The faculty of psychometry is one of the most interesting and instructive of these paranormal powers, and if rightly used it can be of great value.

It is comparatively easy to acquire some ability to psychometrize without any special training, but it is far better, from every point of view, if some definite system of training is undergone by the would-be psychometrist. The faculty so trained is in every way superior to the untrained variety.

The training necessary for the development of the psychometric faculty can be divided into several techniques, and in the next chapter we will deal with these in some detail. However, before we go on, we would like to explain what may have seemed to some of our readers an excessive use of the word faculty. Most people who deal with these things would commonly refer to "psychic powers," but we prefer to use the term faculty as it is a more correct description of them. They are *receptive* faculties, not *expressed powers*.

15

Preliminary Training

WE have already pointed out that it is quite possible to develop the power of psychometry without any training, as, of course was the case with the pioneers in the modern rediscovery of the faculty. Indeed, this holds good of all new discoveries or rediscoveries, for it is only by repeated experiment and classification of the results obtained that the underlying laws of the subject are formulated. It then becomes possible to devise a method of systematic training. However, even when such a system of training has been evolved, it must always be kept in mind that the exercise of these psychic faculties, although based on a true scientific foundation, is also very much of an art, and any system of training must allow for the personal factors involved. A similar state of affairs is to be found in the visual arts; a painter, for instance, may have a very exact mechanical technique of painting, but the real value of his work will lie in the personal element which he puts into his pictures. So it is with this psychic faculty of psychometry.

The Rule of Natural Law

The reference to a scientific basis to psychic practice may surprise many of our readers, who have always understood that these things belonged to a supernatural order of things and were not amenable to scientific law. However, those who have studied these matters most deeply are convinced that they are indeed subject to the rule of natural law. It is necessary perhaps to point out that when we talk of the natural laws of the universe, we are really referring to what has been termed "the predictable sequence of events observed over a long period" and not to the actual immutable cosmic law which is the very framework of this universe. In other words, it is our concept of the true natural law. An example is to be found in the Newtonian hypotheses of gravity and light. Within certain limits these theories work well, and account for most of the observed facts, but there are facts which do not fit into their scheme, whereas the general hypothesis of relativity, as formulated by Einstein, does cover them.

In the same way, the Victorian scientists, forming their hypotheses upon a purely material basis, were convinced that psychic manifestations had no part in the "rational universe" of scientific thought.

"There is no place in the universe for ghosts" declared one of them, and another, "In matter I see the promise and potency of all life." We have made this digression in order to point out that the laws of nature as expressed at any one time may well be superseded by new hypotheses formulated at a later date. All are but theories, hypotheses, built up to express and explain certain facts. Behind them all is the immutable law of the universe, and the truth or falsity of any natural law hypothesis depends upon how closely it approaches true law. The annals of scientific history are crowded with examples of the relative accuracy of the theories evolved by scientific thinkers to account for the observed phenomena of nature.

All hypotheses and statements about natural law are conditioned by our understanding of the facts observed, our personal prejudices, both conscious and subconscious, and the scope and extent of our experience of the subject. This was not always understood by the Victorian scientists or, for that matter, by many scientists today. A short time ago we heard a prominent psychologist declare that no amount of evidence would ever make him entertain the idea of the possibility of extrasensory perception, since to admit such a possibility would destroy the basis of all modern teaching.

A similar blockage exists also in the minds of many religious thinkers, and this shows itself in the tendency to make a hard and fast division between things "sacred" and "secular." It is this mental outlook which has always tended to regard the psychic faculties as being supernatural. We do not subscribe to this belief, for in common with most of those who have worked along these lines, we hold the belief that the only "supernatural" is the One Who is above all Nature because He is its Fount and Origin. We also believe that it is the Will and Purpose of this One which is the true law of the Universe.

So all manifestation, on whatever plane of existence, comes under the natural laws, and should not be termed supernatural. It is usual, therefore, to refer to the psychic faculties as "super-normal." It follows, then, that they come into the realm of scientific observation and method. Equally, much of the testing and investigating which is carried out is anything but scientific, and its extremes at both ends of the mental scale show a similar pigheadedness and an unwillingness to follow the dictum of the great Victorian scientist, Huxley, who said that the true scientist must be prepared to "sit down before Nature as a little child, and follow where she leads." In what we have written here in connection with the training of the psychometric faculty we have tried to avoid the two extremes of intellectual aridity on the one hand and sentimental stupidity on the other.

Example of an Inadequate Reading

You will remember that we gave a brief outline of a psychometry meeting, and we said that the reading given by the psychometrist was one of the better type. We now want to portray a psychometric reading of the poorer variety. You will notice that the statements made are quite evidential, and are recognized by the owner of the article. It is not in the information given, but in its presentation that the weakness lies.

Our psychometrist takes the article and says: "I see a lot of water—there's a man here—I think it is the sea—the man has a queer uniform—I see quite a lot of trees, greyish-green leaves—I have a feeling of Church influence—incense—the trees are growing on low hills behind a town— are you in some doubt as to the best thing to do?—there are Italian influences connected with this article—the man is looking at something—have you been intending to go to Italy?—I get the idea of guns going off—were you in the war?—the man is wearing a sword, he seems to be in command of something—don't worry, the way will be made plain for you in a few days."

Selective Action

You will observe that this reading contains most of the evidential facts given by the first psychometrist, but instead of being a coherent series of statements, it is a mass of jumbled fragments. How does this arise? There are two main factors and one subsidiary one. First of all, it is a peculiarity of the psychic faculties that the information received through them comes into the mind as a solid block of knowledge, and this is then sorted out by the subconscious and projected into the waking consciousness in some kind of sequence. Incidentally, this same kind of thing happens with ordinary physical vision. The eyes present the total picture they are receiving to the visual center in the brain and this results in information being passed through the subconscious into the waking consciousness. Normally, there is a selective action which goes on in the subconscious, and it is this subconscious selective action which breaks up the block of visual impressions received and presents its parts in a particular pattern to the waking self. The subconscious selective action is triggered off by several things. We may have been reading about a river in flood, and the damage it has caused, and then, in the course of the day we are in country conditions in which, among many other things, a river is seen. Almost invariably the first thing we shall notice about the countryside we are looking at will be the river, because our subconscious has been keyed to it by our reading earlier in the day.

Psychological Bias

Here we come to the second factor in the matter of perception. A psychological bias has automatically built up in our subconscious, and all incoming impressions from any of the senses are affected by it on their way to the conscious levels of the mind. If we know what bias we have in any direction, we are able to consciously compensate for it, but if we are unaware of even having such a mental twist, then it is liable to affect our judgment of what we receive through our senses. Particularly is this the case when we have to assess and record what we saw or heard. This is well known in police and legal circles. Two witnesses of the same accident, standing at the time in almost the same place, will give two honest, straightforward accounts of what happened, and these two reports will virtually contradict each other!

This imperfect selection of impressions is obvious in some of the descriptions given by clairvoyants and psychometrists, and is, in large measure, due to lack of good mental training. It is fairly obvious that everything that comes into the mind is recorded in consciousness, and this mental record is the basis of what we call "memory." So the record which is the result of incoming psychic perceptions operates under the same mental laws as the mental record which is made by incoming physical sense perceptions.

The Ability to Observe

In the case of the psychometrist the incoming block of psychic impressions must be recorded and sent out again very quickly, in somewhat the same way as the visual impressions received by a television sports announcer must be put out again immediately as a running commentary on the game he is watching. This means that the selective power of the mind must rapidly select incidents in the game in their correct sequence, and for this process to be carried out successfully, the first ability needed is the ability to observe. This ability to observe in sequence is not as common as some people might imagine. Most of us, because of psychological blind spots, tend to observe some things and not others, or else we confuse the sequence in which things took place. Trained observation is essential for anyone using the psychic senses, and it is the lack of this which we referred to as a subsidiary cause of trouble in psychometric development. The fine psychic impulses received by the psychic must be realized, recorded and translated into vocal or written words. If this is not done almost immediately, these impressions will merge into the general mental field, and become mixed with and distorted by the existing thought images therein.

An essential part of training, therefore, is the cultivation of this power of observation, for, though all impressions are recorded in the mind, they very often never emerge into the waking consciousness but remain below the mental threshold, in the subconscious. It is necessary, therefore, to train the mind to so operate that many more of these incoming impressions are recorded in the waking consciousness. There are various exercises that have been devised to effect this training, but many of them suffer from being far too complex. In all these matters the simpler an exercise can be made to be, the better its chance of success.

Attention and Concentration

Let us consider for a moment what "observation" really is. It is the power to pay concentrated and consciously directed attention to the impressions that are aroused in our minds through the actions of our senses, as those senses react to all the various things and happenings which form the background of our lives. This directed and concentrated attention means that it is necessary to develop the ability to keep the attention fixed on any part of that background at will. This, of course, is what is really meant by concentration. Attention and concentration are both valuable training tools in psychometric development. Indeed, attention is also the key to much successful physical life also, and it should be noticed that the properly trained psychic, whether clairvoyant or psychometric, is not by any means the dreamy, impractical person he is usually thought to be. Of course, there are some psychics who are dreamy and impractical, but we should not judge the great number of psychics by the comparatively small number of impractical freaks to be found in the psychic field. In the cases of many of the freaks, this lack of mental training is one reason for their failure to help or impress the average person.

False Spirituality

It must also be said that there is another and very strong influence at work which tends to encourage such people. This is the emotional and entirely uncritical approach to these matters by so many people. This usually stems from a curious superstition that these faculties are supernatural, and therefore their owners have a license to be freakish. Also there is a continuing tradition that these same faculties are spiritual gifts and many equate the idea of spirituality with vague sentiment, emotion and general "out of this world" behavior. Because of this aura of false spirituality, their followers (for they usually get a following) will also equate the possession of psychic ability with spirituality. This leads to a form of hero-worship in which the unfortunate psychic is placed willy-nilly on a pedestal, and in the eyes of his followers can do no wrong. When finally he does demonstrate that although psychic he is not spiritually developed, most of his followers will immediately kick away the pedestal and abandon him for another hero-figure. A minority of his followers will spend the rest of their lives in attempting to justify him at the bar of their own emotionally biased judgment.

It is for this reason that the genuine psychic needs a training which will enable him to be the master in his own mental sphere, and not dependent upon others. This is what the training in observation, attention and concentration gives to those who attempt it. It produces a mind that can register and sort out the incoming psychic impressions, which are very faint compared with the impressions which are received through the physical senses. Curiously enough, when once the psychometric faculty has been developed and trained, it is possible for these incoming impressions to equal and in some cases exceed the vividness of purely physical sensory perceptions.

The followers of certain occult systems teach that the average person goes through life in a waking dream, responding automatically to conditions around him, and in general justifying the contention of the behavorist psychologists that a human being is but an elaborate piece of mechanism, working by what is termed conditioned reflex. The famous experiment of "Pavlov's dogs" is regarded as proof of this mechanistic view of life, and these occult schools, though entirely disagreeing with the basic materialistic view, nevertheless say that the bulk of the thinking and action of the average man is the result of this "conditioned reflex." However, they definitely teach that it is possible for man to awaken from this dream and begin to act as a conscious being. The further implications of this teaching would lead us too far from our chosen course, but we have mentioned this because it is an undoubted fact that to some extent this dreamlike quality of consciousness does show itself in our waking life and work.

Urban Life Blunts Perception

The conditions of modern life in urban surroundings tend to cause us to react automatically to conditions around us, whereas if we were living in wild natural surroundings, where inattention to the details of life would probably mean our death, we should find ourselves consciously observing everything near us in a way which we should never think of doing in urban life. Every sense impression that came into our mind would be consciously evaluated, and as a result the keenness of our physical sense would be greatly increased.

Even in modern urban life, it would greatly reduce the mortality rate due to accidents if we learned to pay attention to our surroundings, instead of walking or driving almost entirely automatically, depending merely upon the good sense of others, or the speed of our reflexes. This does not mean that we should always be watching our environment with the same intensity as the scout used to have to employ in the days of the Wild West, but it does mean that some part of that quality of intensity must be brought into ordinary life. This, in itself, would not be a bad thing.

Kim's Game

In some of my earlier writings, I mentioned a certain exercise in attention that is commonly known as "Kim's Game," and which was taken from the book *Kim* by Rudyard Kipling. Judging by comments from my readers, this exercise was found by many to be too difficult. Much of this difficulty was, I think, psychological, for when one first starts this exercise, it is usually found to be somewhat disheartening. The reason for this is that it demonstrates

137

very forcibly how poorly we are equipped with the mental power of attention. However, by steady application this particular exercise can develop the power in a reasonably short time. For those who may not have heard of Kim's game, it is played by having a number of small objects, such as rings, colored or carved buttons, small nuts, screws and other small engineering objects all placed upon a tray. For about two or three minutes one directs one's attention upon these things and then the tray is covered with a cloth. One now writes down the names of the objects one remembers seeing on the tray. It is as well if one gets an acquaintance to collect the various objects, but this is not really essential. Having written down as many of the names of the objects as possible, the covering over the tray is removed, and a check made between the total number remembered and the actual number on the tray. As a rough guide, if, out of twenty articles on the tray one can remember eight or nine, then the score is quite good. Mostly about five or six are the best that can be expected. With practice the power of recollection improves until a score of seventeen or eighteen out of twenty is possible.

When a reasonable score has been obtained, the exercise may be varied by attempting to recollect details of each object: its shape, the nature of any carving on it, its color and any flaws that may have been noticed. Those who find that the element of competition helps them may try this exercise as a game, with one or two friends. Mostly, however, we are usually so ashamed of our initial failures that we prefer to play this game solo!

Think Shoelace

Here is another exercise, again a simple one, but very effective none the less. I call it, "Think Shoelace" since it was so described to me by my first teacher in these matters. Briefly it amounts to this: *the attention is fixed upon whatever one may be doing at the moment.* Thus, we are tying our shoelace. Then we simply put the whole of our attention on doing just that. We are not automatically tying the shoelace and at the same time listening, with half an ear to the news on the radio, or the wife's voice as she gives us a list of what we must bring home when we return. Nor are we subjectively wondering what we ought to do at the office, or the plant, in connection with some difficulties that may arise. No, we simply concentrate on tying that shoelace. It sounds so simple that the idea of mental training resulting from it appears farcical, and we are liable to fall into the error of the man in the Bible story who, on being told to wash in the waters of the Jordan to cure his leprosy, indignantly declared that the noted prophet who had given the advice should have done something spectacular: "Stretched out his hand upon me" as he put it, and so made an instantaneous cure. In any case, they had some wonderful rivers, Abana and Pharpar, in his land. Real rivers, not like this little muddy and turbulent Jordan! However, as the story goes, the despised river cured the disease.

This curious desire for the bizarre and spectacular is one which has persisted through the ages, and we will find it in evidence today. It is this taste which causes many people to fall victims to the psychic and occult quacks who are to be found in or around some of the societies and organizations devoted to the study of these matters. The simplicity of this exercise is only apparent. When you have practiced it a few times, you will have become aware of the tricks your mind can play, given an opportunity.

The beauty of this simple exercise is that it can be practiced at any time, without any involved preparation, and the least of its effects is an increased power of concentration, which alone can yield quite a dividend in daily life.

The Faculty of Recollection

A further development is to extend this direct and conscious attention to whatever is happening around us as we catch the bus or train on our way to the factory or the office. How many of my readers, as they read these words, could remember the details of the house at the corner, as they turn from their own street into the main road? Its general appearance, how many windows, its decorations or its front garden (or lack of same)? Again, the people in the bus or train, their appearance, their mannerisms, and so on. How many of us give them any but the slightest attention? Here are the materials for a rewarding mental exercise, and again, it is one which can be practiced at any time. Of course, such attention to other people does not mean that one needs to stare at them, which would be discourteous and could cause trouble, if they objected to being stared at. It is not necessary to stare fixedly for minutes at a time in order to retain a good visual picture of a person or object. This is an important point to remember. As a matter of fact, a quick glance, with concentrated attention, is sufficient. In proof of this, let me give an account of visual recollection given me by a friend who is a hypnotist. He showed someone a page of a book on psychology, having previously found out that psychology was one subject of which the person concerned knew nothing. He then hypnotized her, and when she was in the deep hypnotic state he suggested to her that she was a popular lecturer and was standing on a platform ready to give a talk on the particular aspect of psychology that was touched upon in the page at which she had glanced for one minute only.

She immediately accepted the suggestion and gave quite a good lecturette on what she had read in that brief glance. Where the page did not mention anything on an aspect she talked around it, but where definite statements had been made, she elaborated on them and quoted word for word from the page itself.

This was after only one minute's glance at a page of small print. Incidentally, it is this extremely powerful faculty of recollection possessed by the subconscious mind that so often falsifies what appears at first sight to be evidence of extrasensory perception.

So it is not a question of the amount of time spent in

observing anything or any person, but the intensity of attention which is required.

Presentation of the Evidence

Here we come to a very important point in this training. You will remember that when we described the reading given by a psychic we gave two versions of it, one by a psychometrist of the better kind, the other by one whose work was greatly inferior. We said that it was in the presentation of the evidence that the difference between the two psychics was most apparent, and this links up with what we have just been saying about concentrated attention.

There is a "technique of description," and this technique is not, as a general rule, learned immediately. It involves a disciplined use of the attention, but once gained, it makes all the difference between success and failure. In our opinion, success in this descriptive technique is essential if you wish to carry out any work in this field. A similar technique is used by detectives, and also in the regulation work of the police.

Have you ever considered how you recognize a friend or acquaintance? Probably not, for most of us experience recognition in a subconscious manner, and can seldom say how we do it. It is necessary for us to examine this question fairly carefully. There are, of course, certain salient points in connection with people, that are so strongly emphasized that recognition is often based entirely upon them. Thus, the nose of Cyrano de Bergerac would identify him immediately, as would the crooked back of Richard III (if the Shakespearean image is correct). However, any or all of these most apparent points of recognition may be duplicated, and they are not so good for recognition purposes as some other aspects of the individual.

The Finer Points of Identification

One of these other points, and a very useful one, is the manner in which a person stands and moves. Each one of us has his own particular way of standing and moving which is associated with us in the minds of those whom we meet. In fact, there is what may be described as a whole group of such finer points, the nature of which definitely identifies us as a certain person. Movements of the hands, the fingers and the feet, grimaces that become habitual to us, sudden turns of the head and changing tensions in the muscles of the face, especially around the eyes; all these, and many more, serve to identify us, and it is the identification afforded by these finer points that is very often the best evidence which can be given by the psychometrist.

After this in order of importance comes the actual description of the face and form, the clothes and any points connected with them. Here again, the technique is a very definite one, and the general rule is that there should be coherence in the description given. For instance, the budding psychometrist should not begin a description of the face he is perceiving psychically by stating that "the man has blue eyes and a small wart on his neck." He should start first of all by describing any outstanding feature on the face, such as the large nose of which we have spoken, or the absence of part of one ear, or the absence of one eye. Then he should proceed to describe the face, starting with the color and texture of the hair, whether it is smoothly dressed or sticks up in an unruly fashion. Then the forehead, whether it is broad and high or low and narrow, lined with wrinkles or smooth. The eyebrows thick or thin, bushy or smooth; the eyes, their color, their setting in the face, close together or far apart, lines and sagging muscles around them, deeply set or somewhat protruding; the nose, aquiline, straight or retroussé, broad or thin around the nostrils; the ears, large or small, how set on the head; the cheeks, full and round or sunken, florid or pale, general complexion; moustache and/or beard, type, shape and general color and appearance; mouth and lips, full lips or thin lips; jaw and chin, firm or otherwise, general type of face, round, square or lantern-jawed; neck, thin or thick, long or short.

Automatic Sequence of Attention

All this would seem at first sight to be a very formidable task, but as we always register these and other details every time we look at a person (though the bulk of the detail remains below the threshold of consciousness) it is not the mere registration of the details that calls for some training on the part of the beginner. What is important is the gradual building-up of an *automatic sequence of attention*, so that all the details are stored in their correct pigeonholes in the subconscious, from which they can be drawn in the same sequence.

This technique also applies to the details of the body, the arms and legs, the dress and all connected with it. Obviously, there are certain general characteristics that should be described at the very beginning of the description. The height, general type of body (fat or thin) and any outstanding details such as an artificial leg, are some of these.

Then we come to the more subtle points of stance, etc., which we have already spoken of, and it is here that often the most convincing bits of evidence may be gained. To summarize what we have been saying on this question of accurate description, we would suggest the following general sequence:

1. Estimated height and build of person perceived, together with any outstanding peculiarities, such as an artificial leg or deformity of any kind.

2. Clothing, style and color.

3. Quick detailed description of features, any peculiarities to be noted and described first.

4. Any finer points of identification, mannerisms, and so on.

What we have just given applies to the descriptions of people, but, of course, the same principles apply in the case of landscapes and such general surroundings as may be given. Now that you have the principle involved, you may apply it in your own way. Indeed, in all psychic work, there is an area where the *personal* talents come into play, just as they do in painting and sculpture, for instance. You will remember that we have said that all psychic work is as much an art as a science. Here is where your own individual talent may be employed, and it is here that new discoveries may be made. So don't be afraid to experiment in this field. The outline given is a general one, and as long as you have the principle of sequential description fixed in your mind, you may vary the application in accordance with your own particular slant.

Remember that even with such sequential description, it is possible for you to get into a rigid groove, and this may prevent further progress in your work. So preserve flexibility of mind. Use the techniques, both psychological and psychic, which you have been given here until you are perfectly familiar with them and can rely upon them. Then, as your knowledge and experience grow, you can adapt them to your own individual method of working. Remember always that your subconscious has its own point of view, which does not always agree with that of the waking self, and unless you give this hidden aspect of yourself a chance to express itself, it may begin to work against your efforts. We shall return to this later on.

Control of Emotional Reactions

We come now to another very important factor, namely, the place of emotion in our psychometric work. Very often, as we attempt to psychometrize an article, we find the emotional atmosphere which we are sensing is beginning to flood our mind, and we feel very acutely the sorrow or pain or anger connected with the object. This empathy, or "feeling-with," is of the very essence of psychometric work, but if we allow it to dominate our consciousness, then we lose control of our emotional reactions and so obliterate the fine psychic impressions coming in. A perfect analogy is to be found in the well-known radio phenomenon of oscillation. A radio set may, under certain conditions, not only receive the signals on a particular wave-length, but may also re-radiate them in a distorted form as the piercing whistle or howl with which we are all familiar.

In the same way, it is possible to sense the emotional record of the object you are handling and be so affected by it as to lose all contact with the psychic impressions and simply flounder in a sea of emotion, without realizing that the whole thing is out of focus, and what may be a mild emotional record has been enormously exaggerated by your own reactions. It is well, therefore, to train yourself to control your emotional reactions, and one of the best exercises for this is a very old one. It is simple, too, and consists in making yourself listen to some highly emotional attack upon one of your own pet subjects. Listen to a violent attack upon your political creed; or the same technique can be used on religious, artistic or sociological ideas.

The important thing is that you must not sit and listen in a state of suppressed wrath, but neither must you impose upon yourself a mental state of passive resistance. You must simply listen calmly and attentively to the statements made, assenting or disagreeing with them mentally, not emotionally. Remember that the ideas which seem so repulsive to you are tidings of joy to the one to whom you are listening, and in the same way the ideas which to you seem so self-evidently true are equally repulsive to him. A few experiments along these lines will soon convince you of the part emotion plays in what we are usually pleased to term rational thought. Even in the realm of mathematics, which at one time was thought to be practically the only non-emotional subject, we can find the same emotional bias at work as the different propounders of new systems get into print or fulminate against each other at meetings of learned societies.

Is Training Necessary?

Many people develop the faculty of psychometry without any mental training, and some may ask whether all this training is necessary. The short answer is that it is not absolutely necessary, but it can be of tremendous help.

There are many who have gained the faculty of psychometry without any training, except perhaps that given in a development circle and they can carry out quite good work. However, it often happens that the faculty has been misdirected and employed for purposes which to many of us would appear to be outside the legitimate scope of psychometry. This is particularly the case where it is used in an attempt to contact discarnate people. That this attempt may sometimes be successful, as many years of experience in these fields gives us reason for believing, does not mean that this is always the case, and we deplore the use of the faculty in this way. We are of the opinion that there are other and better ways of effecting such contact, and we would strongly suggest that it is most desirable that this wonderful faculty be taken out of the sectarian religious atmosphere in which it is usually found, and treated in an objective fashion. Equally, and with even more urgency, we would try to rescue it from the base uses made of it by the professional fortune-telling element which infests the fringe of the psychic movement.

16

First Steps

HUMAN nature being what it is, we expect that quite a number of our readers will have turned to this chapter without reading anything that has gone before, which is a pity, but it is not uncommon. However, it gives us the chance to point out that although it is really better to undertake the preliminary training before attempting to do practical work, much of that training can be carried out together with the actual psychometrical work. At the same time, it does impose an extra strain upon the developing psychic, and we would suggest that our would-be psychometrists go back to the work outlined in the previous chapter and begin on that, making occasional experiments in the actual sensing technique.

Such an approach will yield dividends, for the more the mind has been brought under some kind of discipline, the more reliable the psychometrical sensings will be. It will be noted that we speak of "sensing," and this is the best way of describing what happens when one attempts to psychometrize an article. Such sensing is a general impression that is received, and unless the experimenter has the visual or aural forms of perception strongly developed, it will remain simply an impression. Then, as development proceeds, the visual and/or audible images will begin to show themselves. Remember, *all* perception, whether physical or super-physical, is in fact a development of *one* basic set of impressions. On the physical plane, the sense

147

of touch is the basic sense, and each of the five senses is a different kind of "touching." Thus, the rays of light touch the sensitive retina of our eye, causing chemical and electrical changes there and in the optic nerves. These changes are transmitted to the sight-center in the brain, and are there translated into visual impressions. Sound waves striking the ear drum cause movement in the complicated hammer-and-stirrup bones of the ear, and this movement affects the fluid in the canal which also contains many nerve fibers. From these fibers chemical and electrical changes are transmitted to the center in the brain that governs hearing, and are there translated into audible impressions. In just the same way the senses of taste and smell operate, all five senses being based upon the one sense of touch, which was the first sense to emerge in evolutionary time.

The psychic perceptions work in exactly the same way. Actually, the psychic is a single immediate perception, conveying direct knowledge to the self, but as the mind has developed through the specialization of the physical senses, the psychic impressions received are, as a general rule, translated automatically into the physical sense images with which we are familiar.

In the first stages of development, it is this general impression which will be received and you must not be disappointed if for a long time you get such impressions without any visual or audible images. At a much later stage in your development, if you have persevered so far, there will come a time when the pictures and auditory images will give place to a formless perception which, however, will give you all and more than you ever received through the images. At the same time, you will retain the power to use the picture—impressions if you wish.

However, this later stage of development will not as a general rule come for some considerable time after you have started your development, and it may not ever appear unless you yourself aspire to its unfolding. For some of you, such further development may be out of reach, and you would be well advised to stick to and train the "form" type of psychometry.

Although we have said that the impressions give way to images of various kinds, there is always a background of impressional sensing that accompanies the pictures seen or the sounds heard, and this background is important in enabling you to interpret what you perceive. We will return to this question of impressional atmosphere later.

Preparing for a Reading

Now you are ready to commence your actual psychometrical development. What are the main points to be observed? The first, is that for successful work you should be as comfortable as possible. No tight clothing, ill fitting shoes which give pain, no uncomfortable seat; though it is as well if you avoid the other extreme in the matter of seating, for you can be too comfortable.

As far as possible, you should be relaxed physically. A good way to achieve this is to use a combined breathing-and-relaxation exercise such as the following. Sit comfortably, but do not cross the legs; keep the feet firmly on the floor, and take care that the edge of the chair does not catch you just behind the knees and so impede the circulation in your legs. Let your hands rest on your knees. Now take in a deep breath, and breathe out slowly, at the same time quietly fixing your mental attention upon the top of the head, and as you continue to exhale, allow that attention to travel down over all your body, until at the end of the breathing-out it has reached your feet. Now take in another breath and repeat the process. The essence of the exercise is that as you allow your attention to sweep down over the body, so that at every point reached you must also relax the muscles of that part. The success of the exercise is seen when you find that the body as a whole appears to be considerably relaxed.

149

Choosing the Objects

You are now ready to attempt your first reading. This brings us to the question of what objects you should choose for your first experiments, for objects vary greatly in the record that can be obtained from them, and in your early days it is as well if you choose those that give the strongest and most easily read impressions.

Before discussing the kinds of objects, it may be as well to consider where they may be obtained. If you can enlist the aid of one or two friends who can supply them, and who can check up on the accuracy of your reading, you will have a considerable advantage, since you will not have to demonstrate your faculty to people who may be skeptical or even antagonistic to the subject. It is as well, also, that you do not know very much of your friends' private lives, since such prior knowledge may quite easily confuse you, and in any case will detract from the value of whatever you may read from the object.

There are two main "memories" connected with every object. The first is the inherent or personal memory of the object's individual and separate existence. Then there is the "gathered" memory. This is the sum of all the impressions that have been made upon it by its association with human beings, and this will give highly complex memories which need considerable skill to read. Of course, it usually happens that one stratum or another in this composite memory is so powerful that it dominates the rest, and prevents you from going more deeply into the general memory connected with its history. Therefore, in your initial experiments select objects that have either a powerful primary or inherent memory-aura, or that have not passed through many hands. It is best, of course, if the object has been connected with one person only, as it is then unnecessary for you to have to try to sort out the memory layers connected with the various people to whom the object may have belonged. The simpler your initial experiments can be made, the better. Later, as you gain confidence in your powers, you can attempt to psychometrize more difficult objects.

Necklaces usually make good articles for reading, but rings and very small objects are more difficult. Keys are not good objects, for they are apt to pass through several hands; neither are handkerchiefs or other washable articles, for the repeated processes of washing and being handled by others make it difficult to pick up the aura-memory. If you attempt to psychometrize gloves, it is best to turn them inside out, as the outer surfaces will have collected extraneous impressions. Letters are a good source, but if you do experiment with them remember that the envelope has passed through several hands, and is of very little use. You should therefore remove the letter from its envelope before attempting to psychometrize it. Perhaps we may start our description of your first attempts in psychometry by taking the letter as the object used.

Technique of Sensing

You can spread the letter on the table and rest the palm of your hand on it. Or you may just put your fingertips on the signature, or hold the letter to your forehead. It is for you to find for yourself the method that best suits you; every person has his own peculiarity in this matter. Preferably the writer of the letter should not be known to you personally, though it should be possible to obtain some knowledge about him after your reading, as otherwise it will be impossible for you to verify the truth or falsity.

Having taken up the letter, you will now make a simple act of will or intention to the effect that you are going to read the psychic record of this letter. Just a simple intention is all that is necessary; a sufficient indication to your subconsciousness that you wish any incoming impressions which may be picked up to be passed through to your waking self. This is a "trigger action" concerning which we shall say something later. You now quietly wait until you become conscious of new and different impressions coming into your mind. These impressions may remain as simple impressions, or they may be accompanied by vivid pictures and inner sounds. Sometimes the pictures will arise without any surrounding impressions, but whatever you get should be described to the friend who is assisting you by acting as an auditor. Should you be compelled to work without such help, then a good tape-recorder can be used for your description.

You will often feel yourself impelled to react strongly to the impressions you are getting, but if you are wise you will not allow this reaction to flood your field of consciousness and arouse similar conditions in your own self. You may also, and this is a frequent happening in psychometry, receive bodily sensations, indications of illness or accident, and these impressions may be very strong. Never allow them to influence you in any undesirable fashion.

Remember that you are open to all the influences coming from the object you are reading, and that means that you often sense conditions that you do not like, just as you also sense conditions that appeal to you. You must not, however, be selective at this stage in your development, but must allow all the impressions received to come up into consciousness.

At a later date you can be selective, and follow one particular train of psychic images, but at first this is not possible. At the same time you must not allow any undesirable impression to affect you too strongly. When this seems likely to happen, it is best to put down the object and break your contact with it. This is sometimes done by the psychometrist washing his hands before starting to contact another article, but it can also be done by a simple act of will, a definite intention to break the contact.

Necessity for Discrimination

What you often get, and this applies particularly to letters, is the impression of the personality of the owner or writer, and this can be both evidential and useful. Remember, however, if the writer of the letter or the owner of the object has recently suffered a great shock, or has been under considerable mental and emotional strain, then you will in all probability pick up this condition before anything else. So even in the simplest reading, you will find that it is necessary to use a good deal of discrimination, and not to accept all your impressions at their face value. Thought has a very real existence, apart from the mind and emotions that formulated it, and the results of such thinking are often most strongly impressed upon the object, and may well be read by you as impressions of actual occurrences. In the same way, clairvoyants often find it extremely difficult to differentiate between such emotionally charged thought images and actual astral beings or conditions.

This discrimination will develop as you continue to practice psychometry. You will find that you are developing a curious intuition which enables you to perceive the subtle differences between the impressions due to thought and those due to actual physical activity. This subtle perception is something well worth cultivating, as its use can be extended to many other fields of experience.

When describing the impressions you are receiving you should always aim at presenting as balanced a picture as possible. If you must err, then it is best to err on the side of brevity rather than on the side of long-windedness.

Although the psychic impressions are received in the subconscious in a block, you will find that in practice they emerge into the waking consciousness at varying speeds. In some cases you may have to wait for quite a long time before any impression comes through, and such a slow rate of emergence may continue. With other objects you will find that the impressions come pouring through at a very rapid rate. So don't be worried if the impressions seem to "dribble" into your mind, or if, on the other hand, they are so rapid that it seems impossible to make a note of them.

Again, the strength of the personality of the owner of the object will very often force these impressions upon it in such a way that they form the strongest layer of influence connected with it, and they will therefore be the first to be sensed by you.

Increase of Accuracy

It very often happens that the particular health conditions of the owner of the article may be sensed by you so strongly that you actually feel the pains left by him to such an extent that they seem to be actually in your own body. This could be undesirable, unless you deliberately and with intention break the contact with the object you are psychometrizing. In a later section we will suggest to you a method which will enable you to break any particular contact and also to "tune in," as it were, to any aspect of the general block of psychic impressions received from any object. This, however, is best done after you have begun to get some actual results from your experiments. At first you may find that out of ten statements you may make about an object, perhaps two will be more or less accurate, one may bear a relation to the actual state of things, and the rest may be either somewhat near or else far from the mark. With practice, this proportion will gradually change, and as you gain confidence the proportion of hits to misses may be sixteen or seventeen out of twenty. When you have arrived at this stage, you may consider yourself to be quite a good psychometrist.

Keep a record of your experimental work, and record not only the successes but also the failures. Never be afraid to admit that you *have* failures, but use them as means to discover the laws underlying your work. There are psychic tides and currents which will work for you or against you, there are psychic tides within your own inner self which may work with or against the outer tides and influences, and there is also that imponderable factor: the influence of your own personality upon your psychometry. As we have already said, this partakes of the nature of science *and* art. Learn to observe your own reactions to the impressions you receive. You will find that some of them are welcome, others are a barrier. Try to find out why this is; endeavor to understand your personal equation, and above all things, never consciously twist or alter what you receive either to impress others or to excuse yourself.

Presentation of the Reading

Now we wish to touch upon another point. This is how you should present your reading. Sometimes conditions of illness or even death are strongly felt, and you must be extremely careful not to express this impression in a way that might cause the person concerned to auto-suggest themselves into the idea that the condition cannot be altered or that death is inevitable. We have heard some very reprehensible statements made in this way by psychometrists and we would most strongly urge you to give out these impressions in such a way as to give warning of difficulties ahead, together with whatever impressions you may have as to how these difficulties may be surmounted. Remember this: even when you have attained quite a considerable proficiency in this work, you are still far from being able to act as Sir Oracle. In the first stages you most certainly are not in any such position of infallibility.

We are strongly moved to emphasize this point because we have seen how harmful such statements can be. For this reason we urge you to exercise discretion in these things.

Importance of Discretion

Here we touch upon another thing. We have just used the word discretion. Many psychics have a nasty habit of discussing with others the information they have received psychically about other people. This is inexcusable on any count. The attitude of the psychometrist should be

155

that of the doctor or lawyer; whatever he learns through the exercise of his psychic faculty should be regarded as entirely confidential and should not be divulged to any other person. We have seen so much trouble arise through a failure to observe this rule, that we would impress it upon you with all the force in our power. Such malicious or ignorant gossip is one of the reasons why so many cultured and intelligent people are turned away from the whole subject, and these are just the people whom we would wish to become interested.

Selective Working

When you have begun to gain some proficiency in psychometrizing you should begin to employ a "selective" method of working. So far, you have been passively receiving whatever impressions and pictures entered your mind as you read the object. Now you must learn to develop the power to direct your psychic vision in any way you wish. You must actively reach out for the information you desire, instead of passively receiving whatever may come along. Such a power of selection, once acquired, is a distinct step forward in your development and gives you an increasing control over your own faculty.

There are two ways in which this may be done. In the first way a general intention is made by asking a definite question in simple and pictorial terms. The more pictorial it is, the better chance it has of being answered by the psychic faculty of the person concerned. An actual example may help to illustrate this point. If we wish to obtain information along one particular line connected with the object being psychometrized, we take the article and make the usual passive contact with it. As a general rule, there then builds up in our mind a whirling sphere of greyish mist, in which small starry points of light gleam. Each point of light is the starting place of a line of knowledge concerning the object and those linked with it. We now mentally ask the question we have in mind, and at once one of the points of light appears to *become signifi-cant*, and as we look at it, a stream of impressions referring to the question asked begins to pour into our mind.

The Tree of Life

This is one way in which this positive action is brought into play. The second way to achieve selective contact may be by using a "Key Symbol." This symbol has been linked with a particular emotional and mental idea. Thus, a key symbol that could be used could be an orange-colored circle with the symbol of the planet Mercury in its center. This particular symbol is one of a set of ten which together form what is called "The Tree of Life," and this is one of the very important group of symbols used in a certain occult philosophy known as the Qabalah. The symbol of Mercury has special reference to all matters concerning mentality: books, lecturing, conveying information by any means (Mercury or Hermes, as the Greeks called him, was the Messenger of the Gods) such as letters, cables, telegrams or personal conversation. So if it is desired to obtain by psychometrical means some information as to the intellectual caliber of the writer of a letter that is being psychometrized, then this symbol would serve as an excellent key symbol and keep the psychic impressions on track, to the exclusion of irrelevant matters. *But the key symbol must have been thought out and linked in the mind with the characteristic to which it was to be the key.* So you would have to make your own key symbols, though of course you could use the symbol system of the Tree of Life as your basis.

Color Symbolism

There is also the question of color symbolism. You will find that you will receive many impressions of color in connection with objects you psychometrize and in some cases the color will appear quite vividly. There is a general code of color symbols, and this may be found in such a book as *Man, Visible and Invisible,* by Annie Besant and C. W. Leadbeater.

However, you will also discover that your inner self has its own particular meanings attached to various colors, and for you this is much better than relying upon the findings of others. So you will have to work out your own scale of color symbolism, and this in itself will be of considerable value to you in your development. Incidentally, some psychometrists regard strong vibrant colors as relatively "low" and "earthly," and delicate pastel shades as being "high" and "spiritual." Do not fall into this particular trap. The strong vibrant colors are just as "high" as the weak pastel shades. In these matters, you must use your own reason and not slavishly follow others.

Flower Psychometry

There is a curious form of psychometry which is very often demonstrated in public meetings for psychometry. It is usually called "flower psychometry" and the procedure is as follows. The querist brings a flower to the meeting, and this flower is psychometrized in the usual way. Before coming to the meeting, the person concerned takes the flower he has picked (which is the best procedure) or bought (which is not such a good procedure), and holding the flower he considers in his mind any particular problem that is worrying him, and upon which he desires advice.

In a great many cases it is this problem that is picked up by the psychometrist, and the resulting advice may come from his own mental point of view, or be derived from the psychic impressions received from the flower. In any case, the flower has provided a link between the querist and the psychometrist.

The explanation given of this particular method is that around every object there is a psychic atmosphere or "aura." In objects this aura, which carries the records, is complex, as it has been subjected to many influences at various times in its history, and for this reason it is more difficult for the psychometrist to pick up any particular past. But the aura of the flower, which is also a *living* thing, is much more of a blank sheet, a *tabula rasa*, and the strong thought and emotion impressed on it by the querist will be far more easily picked up. The budding psychic may try experiments with floral psychometry, but he should continue to experiment with all kinds of objects, bearing complex psychic records, and not remain content with this elementary method. It is very easy to fall into this trap, but if you do, then you will have limited your psychometric powers considerably, since the use of the triggering key symbols is just as effective as the floral contact and can yield much more information. The main thing to remember is that you should never be content to stay at one level. You should always be pressing forward to greater proficiency, and never be afraid to make experiments. Those which you can think up for yourself will usually prove more fruitful than those suggested by others, as they will usually be the results of some effective thinking that has taken place in your deeper mind. At the same time you should be on the lookout for new suggestions for further experiments.

Let us give you an illustration of what we mean. A number of years ago, we attended a public demonstration of psychometry given by a certain Captain Bland. During this demonstration he showed us an interesting experiment. Instead of holding an object in his hand in order to psychometrize it, he asked the owner of it to place it on a table some ten feet away from him. He then concentrated his attention upon it for a moment and proceeded to give a very evidential reading concerning it. Here an interesting point was raised, for there are those who say that the psychometrist reads the record which is held in the aura of the article, just like the dog which follows a man by the actual scent he leaves upon the ground and upon everything he touches, while others maintain that the object, being by its actual existence linked with all its associated records in the universal mind, itself acts as a link between that part of the universal mind and the mind of the psychometrist, through the images it calls up in his mind. All of which sounds somewhat involved, though if one substitutes the term Akashic Record for universal mind, it is the theory held very largely in the East. The other, which we call the "Bloodhound theory," is perhaps more easily accepted by the average person than the metaphysical oriental idea. Both views are correct, but each needs the other to round it out fully.

Now we come to a more obscure aspect of our subject. When we gave an imaginative description of the average psychometry reading, we included in it a ring which had once been in ecclesiastical hands, and we did this for a definite reason. In an earlier part of this book we referred to three kinds of impressions that it was possible to receive, but later we referred to only two of these. One was the record of the article itself, its basic nature and manufacture. Then came the gathered memories that it had acquired in its use by human beings under differing circumstances.

Charged Objects

There is, however, another set of impressions that an object may carry, and these are impressions that have been deliberately imposed upon it by the will of some being, whether human, sub-human or super-human. Very often the impressions made upon the object partake of the qualities of all three grades of intelligence. Here, of course, we are to some extent touching upon some aspects of being regarded by many moderns as being entirely fictional. Angels and fairies are relegated to the fantasies of childhood, and learned anthropologists spin wonderful theories to explain the records in every part of the world that appear to indicate that forms of life other than those using material bodies have been seen by many people under many different conditions. However, because of our own personal experience in this field, we feel pretty sure that there are good reasons for the continuing belief in the existence of such intelligences.

Here, we are stepping upon the borders of the magical. Anyway, we are going to offer certain ideas and suggest certain experiments which may be of interest to those of you who wish to go beyond the mere giving of psychometrical readings. Perhaps this is the point where we should give the details of an important aspect of your development. If you were concerned with certain chemical work, you would have learned a little trick which often saves the chemist quite a lot of trouble. He may want to know what is in a given bottle or flask from which the label has been removed, and, of course, the natural procedure is to open the bottle and see what it smells like. Here there is a possibility of danger, for the substance may be highly toxic and highly volatile, so that before you can get it out of your lungs you may have been affected by it. The trick is first to take a good deep breath and then, holding that breath in the lungs, take a further sniff at the contents of the bottle. Your lungs, being filled with air, do not take in any quantity of the gas given off by whatever substance is being tested, but enough reaches the olfactory nerves for you to identify it. If it is something very irritating or dangerous, the lungs can immediately be emptied, and the released air sweeps out with it the very small trace of the lethal element which may be in the nose. In the past we have found this little trick has saved us quite a lot of trouble.

We have mentioned it here because your approach to what we propose to call "charged objects" should resemble such a method of dealing with whatever force you may contact in connection with such articles, of which the ring mentioned in our psychometric reading is one. It is very necessary that you approach such objects with the correct attitude of mind. This should be a positive intention to read the record of the object. Then, following this triggering-off action, the mind should be kept receptive, but still positive. This attitude has been described by a Roman Catholic writer, the late Monsignor R. H. Benson as comparable to the flight of a seagull hovering practically motionless against a strong gale. We know that in spite of its apparent immobility, the gull is working very hard indeed to stay in the one place. So the receptive attitude of which we have spoken should also be the "receptive point" of a strong mental intention. This attitude of mind is not acquired at the first attempt, and it is for this reason that we have reserved our treatment of these charged objects until we had given you the more simple and easily acquired techniques.

Incidentally, in case any of our readers are led by our reference to R. H. Benson to think that he became a convert to psychic teachings, we may say that this illustration was used by him in connection with a book of stories on mysticism, and this has very little to do with psychic phenomena. It is true that certain psychic phenomena very often appear in the lives of the mystics, but they are regarded as hindrances, not helps to the mystical life. This, by the way, is true also of Buddhism and some other Oriental religions. They all strongly oppose the development of the psychic powers, which, they say, are like toys which lure a person away from the spiritual path, and at best are time-wasters. The word "mystical" is greatly misused in these modern times, and made to refer to psychic and occult phenomena.

Examples of charged objects are talismans and charms, the virtues of which are extolled in the various psychic and occult publications. Some of these are sold on the well-known dictum of the showman, P.T. Barnum, "There's one born every minute," but others have been carefully made by people who have a good working knowledge of the principles of magic. The first class of charged objects works primarily by auto-suggestion on the part of their possessors, but the second class really has power apart from such auto-suggestion, and it is the objects in this second class that should be approached with caution. If it is known that one has, or is developing, psychic powers, the offering of such an object for a reading is common practice, and it is as well to take due precautions.

We come now to the second class of charged objects and these are those that have been blessed or consecrated by the priests of some Christian and non-Christian bodies. Of such was the ring that our hypothetical querist put up for a psychometric reading. Here the influence radiating from the object is keyed (if the blessing or consecration has been properly carried out, and not in the perfunctory manner characteristic of some ecclesiastics) to a high moral and ethical level, and the effect of it cannot but be helpful.

Even here, however, it is advisable to approach such an object in the same mental attitude as that used in the case of the other type of subject.

An Exercise in Charging Objects

Now we may suggest that you carry out certain experiments of your own in connection with these charged objects. This will require the cooperation of a sympathetic friend, and if this friend has a good power of visualization, so much the better. The exercise is carried out in the following way: five pieces of wood, say about three inches long and an inch wide (thickness immaterial) are taken and marked either by numbers or letters, so that they can be distinguished from each other. The one who is to "charge" them then enters in a notebook exactly what strong emotion he wishes to impress upon each one. As this is best done by visual images, he should also enter in the images he proposes to use in each case. We will suppose that the object marked A is to be charged with the emotion of anger. He may use any image he thinks gives a good picture of this emotion, and, holding the object between his hands, he builds up the picture as strongly as possible, at the same time endeavoring to feel the emotion which it portrays. Having done this, he wraps the object in a piece of silk and turns his attention to the next object. It is advisable, by the way, to allow a period of some fifteen minutes or so for him to clear the emotional bias from his mind, otherwise the influences on the next object will be somewhat mixed.

This work should be carried on until all five objects have been charged. Of course, during this work you should not have been in the same room, nor should you have been within earshot of what was going on. It would be best for you to be out of the house altogether.

Now the objects are handed to you, or you take them up one by one yourself, unwrap them only as you do so, and then give your reading, endeavoring to describe the general emotional effect together with any pictures that may come up. Having dealt with the first article, you pass on to the second, unwrap it and repeat the process, and so on with them all. After each reading, rub your hands vigorously together as though rubbing off dust. Some psychometrists wash their hands after each reading, but this is really unnecessary, and, indeed, is impossible if you are giving a public demonstration. The readings that were given for each object are now compared with the entries made in the notebook by the one who charged them, and successes and failures noted.

This is a very good exercise, for when you begin to be able to sense these different emotions in this way, you are increasing your ability to select just that particular line you wish to follow from out of the mass of information you received from any article.

Once you are able to pick up influences in this way, you can use the faculty to sense the conditions of any room or house you may enter, and this may be helpful to you at a later date.

Person Psychometry

Finally, it is also possible for you to psychometrize a person, by directing your intention toward him and then picking up the images and sensings that come into consciousness. Here is a big field for experimentation. Incidentally, you will find in connection with this "person psychometry" that most people carry around in their aura quite a few definite thought forms, and in some cases these forms have considerable emotional energy locked up in them. Some may be the result of intensive visualization; they may have been reading a gripping and exciting novel, and the characters in the story have been so clearly visualized that they exist in the aura as well defined forms which may easily be picked up by the psychometrist.

Another interesting phenomenon may be experienced in this psychometrizing of persons. Apart from imaginary characters from novels one sometimes sees other forms, which when described by us are usually not recognized by the person concerned. If, however, the form is sufficiently striking in appearance, the person may say "That's got nothing to do with me, but it *is* a very good description of a man who called on us this week, and caused a bit of a row!" The key is in the latter part of that remark. The strong emotional reactions aroused have caused the image of the one concerned to be strongly imprinted on the aura, and so be easily seen and described by the psychometrist. In a later piece dealing with the subject of reading the aura, we hope to go more fully into this and other aspects of what we have called person psychometry.

Diagnostic Psychometry

There is another interesting application of psychometry. This is "diagnostic psychometry." It is an occult teaching that disease in the physical body originates in the subtle "etheric double" which is the background to the physical body, and upon which the physical body is continually being built up and broken down, so that we do not possess the same material body that we had five years ago. (Some medical authorities say two years see a complete exchange of physical matter in the body.) So, according to this occult teaching, the etheric body is the *real* persisting body, which we keep during our entire life, and it is in this body that the first symptoms of disease are to be found, long before any purely physical symptoms are felt or signs seen that can provide material for diagnosis by the doctor. It is during this pre-matter phase that disease may best be dealt with by the more subtle methods of homeopathic medicine and so-called spiritual healing, though of course these methods can be quite successfully applied even when the disease has gained a strong hold on the actual material body.

In this field of psychometry great care is required, for there are many people who can be adversely affected by such a diagnosis because of auto-suggestion on their part, and this can and has led to tragedies in the past. If you should decide to follow this line of work, it would help you greatly if you followed the example of a friend of mine who took a two-year course in anatomy and physiology before commencing.

In the first stages of the development of this phase of psychometry you should move your hand over the subject's body, keeping at least three inches away from actual physical contact with the person. It is never necessary in this diagnostic work to make any physical contact with the body of the person concerned. If you break this rule, then you align yourself with those malpractitioners whose aims are sexual, not psychic, and you will cause yourself untold trouble. For the same reason, if you ever do this kind of work, *always* have a third person present during any interview. We have referred to this form of psychometry, since it is a very interesting phase of the work, but personally speaking, we would not advise you to take it up on any large scale.

Another interesting phase of the work is that of distinguishing fake jewels from the real variety, fake Egyptian antiques made in Japan from the real articles, and fake period furniture and art pieces from those that are genuine. Those who are interested can devise quite a number of experiments in this field.

17

Some Friendly Advice

THE writing of this book has been for us a labor of love. We have derived great satisfaction in putting together some of the knowledge concerning this wonderful faculty which we have gained through some fifty-three years of practical experience in the field. There are few books on the subject, and what there are seem mostly to be written from a sectarian, religious point of view. We have tried in this book to avoid any such approach, since we firmly believe, as we have suggested, that these psychic faculties are in the same category as our other physical plane senses, and do not depend upon our moral or ethical outlook. At the same time, of course, it will have become evident to those who have read so far that there is a definite standard that must be maintained by the would-be psychometrist.

This does not mean that he must belong to any definite religious body, but it does mean that if he is to get the full value out of his work, he must be prepared to discipline himself. The Bible says, "greater is he that controlleth himself than he that taketh a city by arms." This self-control is one of the greatest virtues of the psychometrist, and must, if it is to be really effective, extend over a wide area of his own personal self, and become a powerful factor in his everyday life. Having more control over himself, he finds that he is beginning to have more power over others, and at once certain ethical considerations come into play.

Rules of Conduct

Since he finds himself able to exert power over others around him, he is now faced with the question, what kind of influence are you going to exert on others, and by what authority do you use this influence? There is a saying that power corrupts, and certainly in this field of psychic activity the temptations of power arise, and the more successful in his work the psychic becomes, the greater is the temptation to misuse his power over others.

All the discipline that he has imposed upon himself so far is an emotional and mental control, and it is this discipline which gives him his power. But how shall that power be employed, what rules shall he follow, and what code of conduct shall he apply to himself? All these are questions he must ask himself before he goes any further in his work.

We have carefully avoided any sectarian, religious approach to this purely natural faculty, but now we are compelled to enter the field of religion, for the exercise of these powers, as of every power we possess, is in essence a spiritual thing. There can be no dichotomy; no splitting of life into "spiritual" and "material," for all existence is in the last resort a spiritual thing.

So we may look for some code of conduct, some rules to follow, in the teachings of religion. This is, of course, the age of iconoclasm, the breaking down of all old established images and, of course, the enthronement of new images, for man must have some images, some rules. The old codes are therefore out of favor, but we are going to suggest that they may yet return to power. In the early days of the Russian Revolution, the idea of permissiveness, which seems to be the keynote of today was extended to the whole area of sexual ethics, and the "free love" which is being so fervently advocated by many people today was allowed to flourish. However, the resulting misery and the social disruption consequent upon the application of the free love ethic was such that the Russian rulers revoked this permissiveness and moved back towards the very image which they had in their haste cast down.

We would suggest, therefore, that the code of conduct known as the Ten Commandments is a useful one for anyone who is using these extended powers of the self. The summary of the law, as given by Jesus, is a positive affirmation of this same code, but in the present state of semantic chaos, when the meanings of words seem to be in doubt, perhaps the definite and blunt statements of the old Mosaic code may be more helpful. Other religions have their own ethical codes and such can be of value to the developing psychic. For ourselves, we long ago took the standards laid down by the Master Jesus as our code of conduct, and though on many occasions we must own to having transgressed that code, it yet remains as a guiding line in the difficulties of life, and particularly in the difficulties that arise in the exercise of these super-normal powers of the mind.

Our final word to our readers is, adopt a standard, impose upon yourself a system of self-discipline and then go forward with the development of this power. So will it bring to you, as it has brought to us over the years, happiness and increased opportunities of serving your fellow man.

For in the end, the sole reason for any intensive cultivation of this or any other faculty is the desire to know, in order to serve and that service is to God and his fellow men, and brings some glimpse of that true peace and freedom which come from One who said, "I am amongst you as one who serves."

PART IV

The Aura

18

What Is the Aura?

FOLLOWING my usual custom, I propose to define as well as I can what the aura is. Those of you who have read this book in sequence will have noticed that I usually give the ordinary dictionary definition of the subject, and I do this because it establishes a common ground between my readers and myself.

According to my dictionary, therefore, the aura is defined as "a subtle invisible essence or fluid said to emanate from human and animal bodies, and even from things; a psychic electro-vital, electro-mental effluvium, partaking of both mind and body, hence the atmosphere surrounding a person; character; personality. In a pathological sense meaning a premonitory symptom of epilepsy and hysteria."

I think we may ignore the second part of this definition, though I suppose many would say that anyone who claims to see the aura must himself be subject to hysteria, if to nothing worse! However, as we go on with this study of the aura, I hope you will be reassured, and will not feel that you are being led into hysterical ways of thought and feeling.

The aura is usually seen as a luminous atmosphere around all living things, including what we regard as inanimate matter. Advancing knowledge begins to suggest to the scientist that even in this so-called "dead" matter there are living forces at work, thus supporting the old

Persian poet who wrote of Life as "sleeping in the mineral, dreaming in the plant, awakening in the animal and becoming conscious of itself in man." In many stained glass windows we see representations of Christ and His Apostles in which the aura is portrayed as a surround of golden light. In many cases we only get the nimbus or radiance shown around the head of the figure, but in others it surrounds the whole form. The same pictorial convention is also found in some Buddhist paintings of a very early date. This same way of expressing the spirituality of the person portrayed is to be found in early Hindu and Persian art. A simple explanation of this may be that the artists who originated this conventional way of indicating the moral stature of certain people were themselves able to see this strange phenomenon which has been termed the "aura."

False Auras

The appearance of what seems to be a luminous atmosphere surrounding people has been reported by a very great number of people down the ages. In less critical ages such an aura of light was thought to be a sign of spiritual advancement, but in more modern times it is usually dismissed as either a figment of the imagination or an indication of either mental instability or optical disease. There is some justification for the view that disease of the eye is responsible for such appearances of light around a person, and there is one common cause of illusion in this connection.

It often happens that someone in an audience will remark of a speaker to whom he has been listening intently that his aura was quite perceptible to him. In some cases this may actually have been the case, but often the cause is a purely physical one and has nothing whatever to do with this radiating influence which we call the aura. The explanation is fairly simple. If one gazes with fixed attention at someone for a lengthy period of time, as, for instance, when one is listening to a lecture, the muscles controlling the focusing mechanism of the eyes become fatigued, and the eye focus suddenly alters. When this happens, the new image being received upon the retina falls on a slightly different point, and the result is that the old image is seen as a "surround" to the one we are looking at. This surround will be in the *complementary* colors to that of the person, and will usually be seen as a white or yellow band of light around him. This is purely a physiological phenomenon, but in an exceedingly large number of cases it is taken to be a vision of the aura.

It is important that anyone who is attempting to develop and train extrasensory perceptions should start by cultivating the most scrupulous honesty. It is far too easy to drift into a slack and easy dishonesty and to give vague and sketchy descriptions carefully, though often unconsciously, formulated in such a way as to take advantage of a lack of the critical faculty in those to whom the description is given. This is a very real trap for the unwary and the best remedy to prevent oneself from falling into it is to adopt a high standard of honesty.

This standard is rewarding, for it enables us to trust our vision when we have begun to use it, and this certainty is a valuable thing.

The Field of Force

If we accept the definition the dictionary gives, we see it refers to a "psychic electro-vital and electro-mental effluvium." Let us see just what this means. It is now well established that all the activities of our physical body are associated with electric currents which circulate throughout the organs, and that actually form a definite electrical "field" around us. Russian scientists have recently perfected apparatus which, they claim, can detect this very faint field of force which exists around all living things. They have claimed to detect the presence of such fields extending some twenty-five centimeters from the bodies of some insects. Incidentally, this field of force has nothing at all to do with the electrical charge that is acquired by wearing nylon clothes or using nylon bed sheets. The charge of static electricity which is often built up by friction against such material can give quite a shock. A mild form of this may be seen if a nylon garment is taken off in the dark when the air is dry. The charge is released in a crackling shower of small sparks. This, however, is quite different from the "biological electricity" which is linked with all our bodily activities. So we have in and around us an electrical field of force which may be considered as the first and most dense of the several such fields of force that make up the composite emanation which we call the "aura." Although the term is one that is objected to by those who have had training as physicists, there is a name already in use, the "etheric aura." There is, of course, a still denser aura which is composed of the minute solid particles that are being constantly thrown off from the physical body itself. Such minute particles are left by us upon everything we touch, and go to make up the "scent" by means of which we can be tracked by a dog or other animal. We refer to it here in order to cover the physical aspect of the aura, since these particles also carry with them something of the tenuous substance that is constantly being thrown out from a much finer "body" than the one so many of us regard as the only body we possess.

The True Physical Body

Those who have studied these matters have become convinced, by direct experience in many cases, that we possess a finer body which, although still a physical body, is of an extremely ethereal and tenuous nature. Certain schools of thought refer to this finer physical substance as "pre-matter," and in old occult writings it was referred to as the "astral" substance. In modern occultism that name has been transferred to another type of substance, and this often causes confusion when people read some of the old books and try to understand them under the new descriptions.

This ethereal body is the *true* physical body (it persists from our birth until our death), whereas the coarser dense matter that we usually think of as our material body constantly changes. It has been said that every molecule of our body is changed for a new one within three years, so that there is a constant flow of material particles from this physical body, and a constant replacement by new particles as the forces of what is called metabolism work within us. Metabolism is operating in us in two opposite ways. As the "katabolic force" it breaks down the very complex chemical compounds of our bodies into simpler forms and these are expelled from the body. As the "anabolic force" it builds up from simpler compounds supplied by our food and drink the highly complex compounds that replace those already broken down and eliminated. Thus there is a cycle of breaking down and building up constantly in progress within us. Varying rates and ratios of this metabolic process result in varying conditions of the physical body, and it is one of the chief teachings of occultism that the metabolic processes are initiated from and controlled by the body of finer pre-matter which we term the etheric body. This finer body has received various names. Among the Egyptians of old, it was known as the *Ka*, and in medieval Europe as the *Doppelgänger*. In the East it has been known as the *Linga Sharirah*, in French Spiritism as the *Perisprit* and in various old writings it was known as the "astral body" or "double." In certain Rosicrucian schools it is called the "Vital Body," and this brings us to its particular significance in our study of the aura.

The Etheric Aura

Occultists claim that, as well as controlling the intake and egress of physical material from the body, the etheric body also draws vital energy, or *Prana*, from the sun and other forms of energy from the earth itself, for use in the living economy of the body cells. These energies circulate throughout the etheric body and its dense material counterpart, and having supplied the needs of the organism, they are radiated out from the etheric body in a peculiar haze that extends all around the body for some inches beyond its surface. This haze, which is usually the first part of the aura to be seen, is known as the *etheric aura*. Since the etheric body is so closely connected with all the vital processes of the body, the appearance the etheric aura presents is usually a good guide to the physical health of the person concerned, and the practice of diagnosis by the aura is widespread in occult circles.

I have said that we have more than one body, and we have just been considering the etheric body. Now we come to other bodies, and here the term "body" becomes somewhat misleading. We usually think of a body in terms of the one body with which we are familiar, our dense physical one, but these finer bodies are best described as "vehicles" or "sheaths." In fact, in the East this latter term is used, and they are known as *Koshas*.

It is the practice in certain occult schools to refer to the "emotional body" and the "mental body," and although this is correct from one point of view, I think we may safely say that seldom indeed do we think without some admixture of emotion, and seldom do we react emotionally without some thought entering into the process.

The two aspects of consciousness, emotion and mind, are closely linked together, and the energies of the inner worlds stream through the bodies which are our means of contact with those worlds. These energies also radiate out around the physical body, but over a far larger area than the vital energies of the etheric double. Whereas the extent of those vital radiations can usually be reckoned in inches, the combined emotional-mental radiation extends for several feet in the average person, and in more highly developed people it may exceed this.

The Spiritual Aura

Finally, we come to what we may describe as the "spiritual aura," and here the area over which it extends beyond the body varies from a few feet in the case of un-evolved people, to yards or even miles in the case of highly developed people. It is said in the East that the spiritual aura of the Lord Gautama Buddha extended for two hundred miles, and they also say that the whole of this planet is held in the aura of a very great Being. This is also Christian teaching, though it is usually restricted to the presence of Deity: "In Him we live and move and have our being," as St. Paul says.

It will be clear, from what I have said, that there is not one aura, but several, each with its own peculiarities, working together as a composite atmosphere surrounding us, and being part of the flow of inner energies through all parts of our being. It will also be evident that each level of this aura can only be discerned by an appropriate mode of perception or vision.

Those of my readers to whom this idea of emotional and mental bodies may be somewhat difficult may disregard it for all practical purposes, since, as I have said, these two aspects of consciousness almost always work together in the ordinary person. Nevertheless, the testimony of many clairvoyants is that these bodies or vehicles of consciousness do actually exist. However, they may be disregarded, and attention fixed upon the emanations that stream out beyond the limits of the physical body when we are recording, as we always are, the impressions being received in consciousness from the workings of the senses, both physical and super-physical. Even in states of what we think of as unconsciousness, i.e., in trance, sleep or pathological states due to disease, accident, drug-taking and so on, the aura is still actively engaged in responding to those impressions that are being received from the subconscious levels of our mind, and that part of the aura

179

we have referred to as the etheric aura still shows the fluctuations of the vital forces of the body.

Also, and this is important, the aura is at all times registering the general emotional and mental quality of our consciousness, and this general quality is something which is relatively stable, and is due to a long-continued series of emotional and mental habits of the conscious mind. The result is to give to the aura a certain general coloring which changes comparatively slowly. This basic coloring gives to the clairvoyant a clear indication of the emotional, mental and spiritual character of its owner. This point will be dealt with more fully when I come to the interpretation of the various appearances that are presented to the seer by the action of thought and emotion on the aura.

In the next chapter I want to consider the structure of the aura, since this will give some insight into its character and help you to understand the important part it plays in ordinary life.

19

The Structure of
the Aura

IT must be kept in mind that the aura has two definite aspects. There is what we may call the "form" or "shape" of the aura; the ovoid of colored emanations that surrounds and interpenetrates the physical body, and the underlying currents of energy that cause it to keep this shape. The latter currents may be considered as a magnetic or psychic field of force, through which the finer substances of the inner levels of manifestation are continually flowing.

I have referred in the last chapter to the etheric, emotional and mental emanations that go to make up the totality of the aura, and we may regard these as making up two quite definite constituents thereof. The etheric body is so closely linked with the physical body that we may, for all practical purposes, regard it as the *true* physical body, upon which the gross outer physical form has been molded. As it influences the physical form which we think of as our body, we could also consider the etheric double to be the "inner physical body," and the flesh and blood body to be the "outer physical body." These two are connected by what is usually termed the "silver cord," an allusion to that verse in the Bible which says "Or ever the silver cord be loosened," this being part of a very wonderful statement cast in poetical form describing the process of old age and death.

Those who have developed the faculty of clairvoyance

claim to be able to see this silver cord if they are observing someone who is dying. Briefly, as death approaches, they see a silvery duplicate form leave the dying body, until it is entirely clear of it except for what seems to be a cord or line of silvery light that connects the two bodies. As long as that cord is intact, there is always the possibility of consciousness returning to the material body again, but once the cord breaks, the separation is complete and no such return is possible. The person is "dead."

The Etheric Double

At the same time, the denser part of the etheric body is still connected with the dead physical body, for each individual cell of that body has its etheric independent life, and will continue to live in a purely vegetative manner until the conditions become such that it can no longer function in any way. There is much to be learned concerning the functions exercised by the etheric double, and in these days of organ transplants and the gruesome prospect envisaged by some Russian scientists of idiots being kept alive and used as host bodies to nurture transplants until such spare parts are called for, this is a line of research for those qualified to conduct it which might well be helpful to mankind. The whole phenomenon of "rejection," the mechanism by which the body rejects an alien organ, may turn out to be more complex than is at present realized, and factors other than biochemical ones may be involved.

Indeed, all medical research could be improved if this etheric double was recognized and steps taken to observe its workings. Under such conditions it might be found possible to dispense with much of vivisectional research, which is often misleading, as certain tragic happenings in connection with the manufacture of drugs have made us aware. Also, freedom from dependence upon questionable experiments would be a moral blessing to those medical men who consider that they must use such research in the best interests of their patients, but who feel nevertheless that the methods of research are morally evil.

Of course, one would not for a moment suppose that the possibility of using such etheric vision as a tool of biological research would be considered by the majority of medical men at the present day. However, if the results of etheric research should prove both more satisfactory and more readily applied, then they would be compelled to fall into line with their colleagues. This, of course, is a very long-term idea, but things are moving so rapidly in this present age that it is unwise to set any limits as to what might or might not be done in the near future.

Disease Indicated by Etheric Aura

What we have called the etheric aura is the general radiation, the field of force of the etheric body, and it indicates what the conditions in that body are. Since the etheric directly controls and affects the physical body, it often happens that disease is indicated by the etheric aura long before it becomes evident in the physical and it is in this etheric body that the real remedial action begins. If the indications can be seen in the etheric aura, then it is possible to treat them on that level, and much of the faith-healing, psychic and spiritual healing, takes place in this region of the human being. Because the etheric aura accurately indicates disease conditions that are either latent in the etheric body or have already begun to manifest on the physical levels, it has often been termed the "health aura."

The Dual Etheric Aura

Observations carried out on this health aura have disclosed some very interesting facts. Its general appearance is that of a surround of fine hair-like emanations which form a rough oval around the physical body. The shape of this ovoid often indicates ill-health, by being bulgy or by other departures from the shape taken by the aura of a person in good health. I have referred to this oval of the etheric aura as though it were a simple thing, but further research has shown that so far from being simple in appearance, it is somewhat complex, and some of these complexities are of the greatest interest. The etheric aura of a person is actually dual, comprising an "outer" and an "inner" part.

There is an inner aura that follows the general shape of the body, and is about three or four inches (this is somewhat variable) from its surface. Then there is an outer aura which extends to about a foot from the body, though this distance is more variable than in the case of the inner aura. Even this is not the totality of the aura, for under favorable conditions there is seen an aura, much finer and less easily detected, which extends far out from the surface of the outer aspect of the general aura. This does not seem to have any definite boundary at all, and it may be due to some action by the organized aura of the individual upon the general etheric atmosphere, in somewhat the same way as an electrified body will induce electrical activity in surrounding objects.

Rays of Light

Another interesting phenomenon connected with the etheric aura is the occasional appearance within it of what seem to be rays or shafts of light which in most cases appear to start from the physical body and then ray out into the space around. In some cases it has been noticed that such rays passed to someone or something near at hand, and it was ascertained that the person whose aura was being studied was, in fact, thinking strongly of that person or object to which the auric ray had gone. It may be that we have here one aspect of a telepathic transmission of feeling and thought. However, I shall try to deal with the question of the role of the aura in telepathy later on in this book.

We come now to another interesting aspect of the aura. This is what is commonly termed the "dark space." It is from one-sixteenth to a quarter of an inch in thickness, and exactly follows the outline of the body. All the auras appear to start from this dark space, which I think may be the actual surface of the etheric body itself. Of course, it could be a still further part of the aura, but research has not yet determined the exact part it plays.

Finally there is an aura that is due to the biological actions taking place in the body and in the skin. These result in the generation of a minute electromagnetic field around the physical body, and this can be measured by the use of sensitive instruments. It appears to be increased when strong light falls upon the surface of the body, and different types of light, ultra-violet, infra-red and the primary colors, have varying effects on this field.

The Etheric Skin

So much for the general description of the aura as it is seen by a good clairvoyant, or by the use of the "Kilner Screens." Both the inner and outer auras appear to have a surface skin, and these etheric skins play an important part in the actual health of the individual. When they are observed closely, they are found to be made up of innumerable etheric lines of force, almost as though the ends of the striations or hairlike lines that make up the aura were twisted together to form a covering and protective envelope to the entire aura.

Etheric Leakage

In a normal person in good health, the etheric skin presents an unbroken surface, but for many reasons this is the ideal rather than the actual state of things. In most people there appear to be what can best be described as wounds and tears in it, and these appear to allow for what we may term "etheric leakage." Such open areas in the aura were well known to those who studied these matters in the past, and they called them "orbicular wounds." Certain practices in connection with mediumship can, sometimes, cause such orbicular wounds, and for this reason the older occultists were not altogether in favor of the indiscriminate development of mediumship. Many of the more thoughtful spiritualists at the present time have come to the same conclusion.

Anyway, the orbicular wound was taken seriously by the old occultists, and, I think, with good reason. One of the most serious results of such a leaking aura is that vitality is quickly lost, and the unfortunate person concerned goes through life in a thoroughly devitalized condition, and thus has little energy to attempt any work, and little power to resist the onset of disease. If the etheric vitality is low, then the metabolism of the body will suffer, and under these circumstances the build-up of anti-bodies, which will prevent the onset of disease, is sadly curtailed. So the unfortunate person will succumb to diseases which will only slightly affect his more robust and healthy brother.

Psychic Vampirism

Not only will the vital energy pour out from the aura of one who has sustained the orbicular wound. Its flow can be considerably increased by the "vampire action" of certain people who can only maintain a normal amount of vital energy by drawing it continually from others around them. In most cases this psychic vampirism is a purely unconscious happening, and the psychic vampires would be horrified to learn that they were doing it. Most of us have met, at one time or another, people who depleted one by their presence. Often they are sincere and dedicated seekers after spiritual truth, but the fact remains that anyone coming in close contact with them for half an hour or so leaves feeling that he has been drained of all vitality. (Conversely, the one who has drained him of energy in this way may be heard to say that he really enjoys a visit from Mr. So-and-So, he feels so much better after he has been to visit him!)

Apart, however, from this depletion, there is a corresponding suction, as it were, on their part, as the depleted vital body attempts to recharge itself. But because of the wound in the auric skin, instead of the new vitality being drawn in through the correct and normal channels, it is drawn in from whatever happens to be around in the way of etheric energy. As the sources of such energy may be neither normal nor desirable, the net result of this may be the recharging of the body with polluted and undesirable forces, and these may bring with them the conditions that will predispose them to disease.

Etheric Parasites

Just as physical sojourn in undesirable places and conditions may cause one to collect parasites of different kinds, such as bugs, fleas and lice, so the undesirable forms of psychic life that exist in physical conditions of dirt and neglect will be picked up and become parasites on the etheric aura, where they may be seen by anyone possessing the slightest degree of clairvoyant power.

These etheric parasites appear to be simple forms of life which, in their own place and under their own normal conditions, have a definite part to play in the etheric realm. In this realm there are to be found many grades of living intelligences, as well as a great deal of "throw-out" psychic material which is ultimately dealt with by the purifying processes that are continually at work in these levels, and is then returned to normal etheric circulation. Here, too, there are great currents of energy that sweep through the whole realm and act upon the physical plane in many subtle ways.

These currents, known in the East as the *Tatvas*,

appear to be closely connected with the activity of the sun, and to be somehow concerned with the basic nature of physical matter; that is, its appearance in solid, liquid, gaseous and radiant forms (corresponding to the old alchemical idea of the four elements of Earth, Air, Fire, and Water).

Here in this etheric realm lie the keys to medicine, psychology and psychism, and anyone who submits to the arduous training required to develop and organize his etheric awareness will find a rich field of research which so far has only been explored on a small scale.

Psychedelic Drugs

Certain forms of unwise psychic and mediumistic development will cause an orbicular wound, and this can also be the end result of the use of alcohol in excessive quantities, as well as being quite commonly the cause of the mental and emotional deterioration shown by those who have become drug addicts. This is especially the case with those who have become habitually conditioned to the use of some of the so-called psychedelic drugs such as LSD. Incidentally, this is a realm of action where emotional prejudices are rife, and it is not fair to· say that all drugs cause mental deterioration. However, for anyone desiring to become psychically aware, and proposing to use these drugs for the purpose, the best advice would be that given in the pages of the magazine *Punch* many years ago. Answering a query, "should I marry?", it gave the general advice DON'T. This advice certainly holds good where the psychedelic drugs are concerned. There are better ways of expanding consciousness than these, though they take longer to produce the desired effect. In these days of instant coffee, instant cooking, instant quite a lot of other things, there seems to be a demand for "instant psychic ability." In some rare cases, where the psychic make-up of the person is of a certain type, the psychic abilities may be developed in such a short time that we might speak of instant psychism, but this is not the general rule, and even where it is, the newly developed faculty needs long and careful training before it can be used to the best advantage.

The etheric body is constantly receiving its energy from two sources with which I will deal presently, but it will tend to draw upon the energy of other people if for any reason the vitality pressure is low and there exists this wound in the aura that allows the vital energy to leak away.

Vital Energy

There are people who appear to draw the vital energy from its normal sources in such abundance that, when their own organisms have received all that they need, there is a considerable surplus remaining, and this charges their auras, and rays out as a steady stream of vital energy to all around. Such people are sometimes to be found in the nursing profession, and their mere presence in the room will stimulate the vital forces of their patients. This is vaguely realized by many people, who will say of such a nurse, "She gives you strength when she is near you." Others, equally dedicated to healing, produce no such result, for in their case they seem to be drawing in just sufficient vital energy to supply their own needs.

I have referred to the vampire activities of some people, and have pointed out that in many cases such people are quite unaware of the results they produce upon those around them. It will be seen from what I have said that in both the vampire and his victim there is a lack of vital energy. In the vampire type, the etheric aura reaches out as it were, and draws from others the extra energy it requires. In the victims the lack of vital energy causes a "vitality vacuum" and they will also tend to draw into their aura any surplus energy that may be available. There are many such sources, some good and some bad, and it is unfortunately the case that as a general rule the person who possesses the orbicular wound, or the leaky aura, tends to draw extra energy from organized life units of a lower type, such as certain animals, or from others who are even more negative than themselves, such as very small children. There are much better sources from which they could draw the extra vitality they require, one of which is the etheric aura of living plants, more particularly trees of a certain kind.

A great deal of private research has been carried out into this interesting aspect of the subject, and I shall give you some instructions that you may find to be of great use when and if you ever find yourself depleted of vitality.

Of course, in the case of someone who has a leaky aura, the obvious thing to do is to plug up the leak. Unfortunately such a simple solution is seldom thought of, let alone put into practice, possibly because it *is* so very obvious. Instead, vital energy is pumped into the person concerned, only to be lost almost immediately, and a fresh recharge becomes necessary.

The whole subject of this auric skin or envelope is one that presents fascinating problems for those who desire to understand more of the mysterious way in which our consciousness makes contact with our physical body and brain mechanism. This area of research also permits the application of the scientific method of study in a way that is much more difficult in the case of the emotional and mental levels of consciousness.

Be it noted, however, that this etheric aura and the etheric body from which it emanates is strongly affected by personal thought or that of other people, and since the etheric is the controlling level from which the physical is directed, we have here a clue to the success of some metaphysical systems of healing.

Very many carefully controlled experiments in hypnosis, together with the accounts of spontaneous phenomena such as the alleged "stigmata" (the reproduction of the wounds of Christ which have been seen to appear on the bodies of some Christian saints, St. Francis of Assisi being an example), together with many well authenticated accounts of firewalking and other exploits of some Eastern ascetics, as well as the physical phenomena of spiritualism, all suggest that this etheric body and its aura play an im-

portant part in what is usually termed *supernatural* manifestation, but which should more correctly be termed
super-normal manifestation.

Without going into the vexed question of the proofs
of personal survival, we can at least say that here in this
borderland between the physical and the more tenuous
levels of the emotional-mental worlds, there is a promising
field for the students of psychical research hitherto somewhat neglected.

20

The Circuit of Force

IN order to prevent the previous chapter from becoming too long I decided to deal with further aspects of the structure of the aura in this chapter. I have used the title "The Circuit of Force" since what I have to say is very largely concerned with the flow of energy through the etheric aura. I have already touched upon one of the pathologies of the aura, the leaky aura or auric wound, and I think that what I have to say here may help the reader to see how such a wound may be healed and, what is better still, how it may be prevented from happening at all.

First of all, it may be helpful if we consider what this auric energy is, and whence it is derived. Here we come up against certain established teachings that have in the past been taken very much for granted by many students of occultism, particularly by followers of general theosophical teaching. In some fairly important respects such teaching differs from that given in the Western esoteric school, and from that given in the Eastern esoteric schools. In a way, this is all to the good, for to find the authorities differing may help the enquirer to keep his mind open to new outlooks and teachings. In the same way, to use the illustration of the present state of astronomical knowledge, there is a decided difference between the advocates of what is called the "big bang" theory of the beginning of this universe, and the opposite theory of the "steady state universe," and the efforts of each side to prove their hypothesis to be the correct one are having the effect of rapidly increasing our general knowledge of the universe in many other aspects, entirely apart from its origins.

So, in this difference in the teachings, there is room for independent research, and for this reason, though I shall put forward the general teaching which I have myself received, I shall endeavor to compare it with that given from other sources of which I have spoken, and will describe some of my own observations in this field. Then those of you who may yourselves develop the power to observe the aura will feel free to make your own experiments without worrying about whether your results agree with those recorded by theosophical seers, Eastern yogis, spiritualist psychics and mediums or even those personal observations recorded by me in this and other books!

Chakras or "Centers"

The general occult teaching is that the etheric body draws vitality from the sun and distributes it to the various parts of the body. Another teaching, the Western esoteric one, teaches that the etheric body is drawing energy not only from the sun but from the earth as well. This Western teaching, which I consider to be a fuller exposition of what happens in this drawing in of vitality, affirms that there are certain points within the etheric body, all located along the spinal column, through which this dual stream of vitality is passed into the physical body. This is also taught in the other school, but the nature and number of these distribution points or *chakras*, as they are termed in the East, are differently described in the two systems. In the ordinary theosophical teaching, there are said to be seven of these *chakras* or 'centers,' namely, the center above the head, known generally as the "thousand-petaled lotus," the center between the eyes, the throat center, the heart center, the solar plexus center, the spleen center and the sacral center at the base of the spine.

In the Western teaching, the centers are given as the center above the head, the center at the throat, the heart center, the sex center, the center below the feet. (In both systems the center above the head is located in that part of the aura that extends above the head, and in the Western system, the center below the feet is also said to be in that part of the aura that extends downward below the soles of the feet.) It will be seen that whereas the general theosophical teaching speaks of seven centers, the Western system speaks of only five. In the Eastern Tantric system we have the centers as given in the theosophical teaching, with the exception that the spleen center is not mentioned, and its place is taken by the sex center.

When I was in India, I did a fair amount of practical work in connection with occult matters as a member of a small group of advanced occultists, and in the teaching I received there, there is, I think, the answer to this apparent discrepancy between the systems. We were taught, and it was demonstrated to us, that there were very many such centers in the etheric body, and certain people tended to concentrate upon some of these and ignore others. All, it was taught, were part of an intricate system of etheric channels through which the life forces, including the vital force known as prana, were constantly circulating. The reasons why certain people tended to use a center that others apparently did not worry about were complex, and it was best, so our mentors said, to find out for oneself which was the natural combination of centers for us personally, and to leave our neighbor to work on his own combination. Further personal research, together with the reported findings of many other psychics has confirmed this, and I would simply advise any of you who may worry about these differences to work along those lines and follow those teachings which seem to be helpful to you.

Tantric Practices

We were told that the substitution of the spleen center for the sex center in the theosophical teaching was largely due to a certain unconscious bias against any inclusion of sexual ideas in the matter, since, in the case of certain *debased* Tantric practices, and certain *debased* witch-cult practices the sexual element had been grossly emphasized.

You will notice that I have italicized the word 'debased'. This is because I once received an indignant letter accusing me of being unfair when I referred to "debased Tantric practice" in one of my former books. The trouble was, I had not emphasized the word "debased," and my critic was under the impression that I was attacking the entire Tantric system, which I most assuredly was not. It is a lofty Eastern system of practical philosophy and can no more be blamed for the excessess of some practitioners of Tantric magic than can the Christian churches be blamed for the occasional Black Mass that one hears about now and then.

Western Classification of Centers

The Western classification is quite in line with the general theosophical one if the center above the head is regarded as the one that draws in energy from the sun, and if it is also thought of as being the cause of the lesser center located between the eyes. The cardiac and solar plexus centers together will then form the center located in that part of the body, and the generative center can be considered in conjunction with the center at the base of the spine as one. So we have only lost the spleen center, and it may be that this particular center has other functions. It has been observed that in some cases where the etheric body temporarily left the physical, it apparently used the spleen center as its gate of exit.

We are now reduced to the five centers referred to in the Western teaching. I'm sorry if this upsets anyone who feels that the mystic number seven has been thrown into the discard. Personally, I do not feel that there is any mystic virtue in the number seven, at least as far as this subject is concerned, whatever its significance may be in the fields of numerology and symbolism, but, of course, I may be mistaken! If so, then I must ask the reader's pardon.

The centers that are apparently located along the spine appears to extend out to the surface of the aura in what seem to look like cones or trumpet-shaped vortices of energy, and where these vortices touch the outer skin of the aura, they are covered by what looks like a fine and tenuous web of etheric substance. These vortices are constantly in a spinning motion, and according to the direction of their spin, so energy appears to be drawn in or directed out.

In the system which I am now working with, the center above the head is regarded as drawing energy from the sun, and this energy when so drawn in charges up the solar plexus center strongly. But here we come to a difficult point in our observations. The point at issue is, whether this solar energy, which is specialized by the solar plexus center is the entire energy intake, or is it simply a stimulating and triggering charge that causes an increased amount of vital power to be drawn from the great primary current of energy which comes into the etheric from the etheric world itself by way of the center·that lies below the feet in the aura?

Mental and Emotional Stimulus

In any case, when the solar plexus center is in action in this way, it distributes its energy to all the other centers. Equally, the head, throat and generative centers appear to be stimulated by certain types of energy which they draw from the etheric levels, quite apart from the general vitality distributed to them from the solar plexus. Here I must touch upon something which is, I think, not sufficiently realized by many who work along occult lines. This is that these centers can be stimulated into full activity not only by energies from the sun and other sources, but also by mental and emotional stimulus, such as ritual, the cinema and theater, the television screen or any book so written that it builds up clear and well defined images in the mind of its reader and also stimulates the emotions. I feel that this is an important aspect of this auric mechanism, and the implications thereof in our lives may be far more powerful than we at present realize.

Wounding the Aura

I have been describing something of what happens as the centers draw in energy. What happens when they reverse their spin and begin to pour out energy? First of all, the fine web over the outside end of the vortices acts as an automatic check upon the amount of energy that may be projected and so prevents the individual from losing energy to a dangerous extent. So long as this restraining web is undamaged, this automatic restraint on the vital forces acts efficiently, but there are conditions that may arise when it is damaged, and then we have the auric wound. Certain unwise meditation procedures can do this, but one of the most certain ways of causing such a wound is by the continued practice of drug-taking. Whatever some advanced psychologists may say, the continued use of drugs does do great damage to the aura, and opens it to all manner of invading influences.

The occasional "trip" under careful medical supervision may not have this effect, but I am in entire agreement with one of the most experienced writers in this field, and one who can speak from his own personal knowledge. Dr. I. F. Regardie, writing of the effect of such practices, says ". . . the outright psychotic person . . . should be sternly counseled never, under any circumstances, to touch the psychedelic drugs." Here he is speaking of the psychological states, and, of course, it is realized by most people who have studied this matter that few people are free from some trace of the neurotic or psychotic in their mental make-up. More fully does this apply when we are considering the etheric aura, for therein are many dim shapes that foreshadow coming trouble and conflict in both the mind and the body, for all disorders of the mind, emotions and physical body show their traces in this aura before ever they are made manifest in psychological or physical illness.

To open the surface of the aura to the play of all kinds of forces is equivalent to peeling off the protecting skin from one's body, and the dangers are as great in the one case as they would be in the other. Obviously, no one in his senses would deprive himself of his bodily skin, but because the process is not so painful, there are many who perform the psychic equivalent of this process by practices of various kinds. Some theosophical writers would include tobacco and alcohol under this heading, and it is true that the social use of alcoholic beverages has blinded many to the grim fact that addiction to alcohol is in itself a disease, with distressing consequences. However, the school to which I subscribe does not lay down arbitrary rulings on these points, contenting itself by pointing out that if you want the best results, then you must provide the best conditions!

The etheric web not only restricts the amount of energy that may be poured out from the centers, but it also acts as a barrier to outer influences that may seek to penetrate into the etheric body. As long as it is kept intact, then the possibilities of what I term "psychic infection" are lessened.

Recharging the Etheric "Batteries"

The energies of the various centers may be projected from the aura, and such projections of power are often to be seen as either misty, cloud-like emanations or clearcut rays or beams of light. Much depends upon the intensity of the will or desire that lies behind such a projection of energy. Where the intensity is great, it would seem that much concentrated power may be given out in a short time, and such expenditure of energy leaves the person depleted in vitality. Under these conditions he may tend to become so negative that a kind of suction is established, and he tends to draw energy from those around him or from any convenient source of such power. Here I may mention one method by which such a temporarily devitalized person may rapidly recharge the etheric "batteries."

Vitality is by no means confined to the animal and human kingdoms, of course, but most people do not realize that the members of the vegetable kingdom not only draw in etheric energy, but are also surrounded by a simple aura of such energy which is surplus to their requirements. The quality of these auras varies considerably, but there are some that blend very well with the specialized human etheric energies, and it is possible for anyone who is depleted of vitality to rapidly recharge by a simple technique.

The best trees to choose for this purpose are the pine and fir trees, oak, beech and apple being good second choices. On the grounds of the cottage in which I am writing this, we have a huge oak, several hundred years old, and the aura that it emanates is very helpful indeed. The elm is a tree to avoid as far as its auric atmosphere is concerned, for quite apart from its nasty habit of dropping a dead branch without any warning, it does seem to be in some way inimical to human beings.

However, we will imagine that you have found a suitable pine tree for your recharging activities. You now seat yourself on the ground with your back firmly against the trunk of the tree. Since the ground is liable to be damp, a good waterproof cushion is indicated, and it does not matter whether it is made of rubber, plastic foam or any other material, as long as it keeps you clear of the damp ground. There has been a good deal of nonsense written and spoken about this. Many people subscribe to the superstition that anything made of rubber or plastic will insulate you from the etheric forces. This is just not so, as has so often been demonstrated. Water diviners who believed that rubber neutralized their powers, found that this was indeed the case, but other water diviners who did not believe in this insulating power of rubber were able to divine while wearing rubber soled shoes. The superstition arose, I think, because rubber *is* an insulator as far as electrical currents are concerned, and so led to the idea that the vital currents are electrical in their nature. They are, of course, but in quite a different way, and normal rubber insulation does not cut them off or interfere with their activity in any way, *unless the person concerned thinks that it will have this effect.*

Having seated yourself quite comfortably with your back firmly pressed against the tree trunk, you now adopt a certain attitude of mind, or rather of mind *and feeling.* For in this realm the feelings are important, you don't "think" yourself into the tree aura, you "feel" yourself into it, which is quite a different matter, and one which is not so easy for many people. It is an affectionate feeling toward the simple intelligence that one might figuratively term the "spirit of the tree" which is required. It is a feeling, not a sharply defined mental picture which is required, but a good auxiliary to this feeling approach is to visualize as clearly as one can whatever symbolic form we feel may best represent to us the essential nature of the tree. If by any chance you have developed the etheric sight, then it may well be that you do actually get a glimpse of the living intelligence of which the tree is the outward and visible manifestation.

Now, without strain, but utterly relaxed in this affectionate approach to the living being which is the real tree, you simply rest, and allow the energies that are being given off by it to pass into yourself. Fifteen minutes or even less of this can effectively recharge the vitality batteries in you. On many occasions I have used this method of renewing energy, and I know from personal experience that it really does work. Many others have also used the method, and received benefit from it. However, the key to the whole operation is the feeling rather than the thinking approach to it. It even works with some who totally disbelieve in the possibility of such a vitality transfer, people who put it all down to mere auto-suggestion. You are free to adopt this explanation if it pleases you, but I can assure you that there is more than "mere" auto-suggestion involved in the practice.

Emanations from the Mineral Kingdom

It is also possible to become en rapport with the emanations that are continually being radiated from the mineral kingdom, the rocks and earth around us and upon which we live and move, though the artificial concrete jungle of our large cities often prevents us from receiving these emanations except in a diluted form. At the same time, it is here in the basic etheric of the planet that we make contact, through the center below the feet, with the great sources of vital energy, just as in the center which is above the head we make contact with the positive forces that are the driving energies of the universe on its higher levels.

The Vital Flow

We may think of these two centers as being the two terminals that connect us to the bipolar universe of force and form. These two centers may therefore be regarded as the two terminals of a circuit carrying an alternating current of electricity. You will see that the full flow will be hindered if either terminal is not properly connected to the universal supply.

I have said that this vital flow is an alternating one, going first in one direction and then in another, and anyone who does any practical occult or psychic work has to reckon with the direction of this flow at any particular time. In the East, this has been carefully worked out, but in the West there is not much detailed knowledge available except in some of the more hidden occult groups. Modern psychology, and more particularly what is now called depth psychology, has a good deal to tell us concerning this vital flow and the ways in which it may be checked and interfered with on the one hand, and increased and helped on the other.

According to the direction of the flow of this primary or central current of the aura, will be the nature and manifestation of the universal energy. If it is flowing from the earth center upward, it will tend to intensify the bodily vitality and all the normal functions of the body will be strengthened. If, on the other hand, it is flowing from the head center, then the mental aspects will predominate. But at all times, the aura will be charged with a mixed magnetism, and the ultimate deciding factor in how that power manifests will lie in the hands of the waking consciousness. Though the inner forces may be stimulating aspects of our nature that we find it inconvenient or wrong to express in their basic form at the time, it is the waking consciousness that has the responsibility as to how those forces do actually show themselves in daily life.

It is here in the non-dimensional consciousness of the present that our real development always takes place. For the past is gone, the future has not yet emerged, and only the razor-edged present is ours to work with. Even as we think and speak and act, that which was present becomes the past, and the future becomes the present. Perhaps there is a profound psychological truth contained in the biblical words: "Now is the acceptable time; now is the day of salvation."

The Secondary Circuit

This brings me to another point. The action of this central circuit of force builds up a secondary field of force in what we have here considered as the etheric aura, and this aura has certain phases through which it has to pass. This secondary circuit is sensitive to any outside influences that may affect it, especially before it is properly developed and when it is in a condition which, to go back to our analogy of the skin, is similar to the condition of a physical body deprived of its protecting skin. Thus, this extreme sensitivity is entirely out of the control of the person concerned, and his reactions to those outside influences are correspondingly intense and irrational.

"Open" Psychics

As the general development of the individual consciousness continues, the etheric web or skin becomes more properly organized and begins to shut off the aura from many of the influences that once affected it so strongly. But where this does not happen the individual remains open to all the various outside influences that may play upon him. This is one of the dangers that threaten those who are sometimes called negative psychics. The term has been unfairly used by some occultists to include all those psychics of a different way of thinking to their own, but I am using it here for what has often been described as the open psychic. These open psychics are the curse of any movement in which they happen to be, for with their inability to shut off unwanted influences they are like human Aeolian harps, upon which every passing wind makes sound, usually discordant.

Just as they are receptive to all influences that strike upon their aura, so are they open to every predatory influence that may desire to draw from them what vital energies they may have to give, though as a general rule, because of this leaking aura, the amount of vitality they are capable of losing in this way is small, since there is never a large supply in store.

With true development, however, the aura becomes insulated against such involuntary reactions, and the etheric centers begin to be capable of being used as perceptive organs under voluntary control.

A wide field of interesting research lies before the clairvoyant who elects to work along these lines, and it is my own considered opinion that this research may well be of great use not only in what we may call the psychic field, but in the fields of medicine and electronic physics as well. Some interesting experiments have already been made into the nature of electric currents, using the developed etheric clairvoyance of one member of a research group, but owing to the mental reactions of orthodox workers in this field, the work of this particular group has been suspended, for the time being at least. However, it may well be that some time in the future the intellectual climate may so change that this type of research will be again carried out.

The etheric aura is not only a surround or atmosphere that is the basis of the physical body. It not only receives influences but also sends them out. The influences that are sent out from the etheric aura are of various kinds, and are capable of considerable variations in both strength and quality. Normally, the healthy person, and by healthy I mean psychically and mentally, is constantly radiating a steady flow of etheric energies during the waking state, and this personally colored force constitutes what we may call the personal magnetism of the man. There is also a steady flow of vital energy from the healthy person, for he draws into himself more than enough of the vitalizing forces of nature, and the excess left after his physical body has used all it requires is radiated out in a steady stream.

Etheric Healing

Many healers work with this vital energy and are able to recharge those who may, for one reason or another, be depleted. There are, of course, grades of this vital energy, and for this reason various healers appear to work in different ways. There is one important thing to remember about this use of the excess vital energies for the purpose of healing. When Dr. Mesmer, who popularized this form of healing in France during the latter part of the eighteenth century, put forward his theories as to the energy that he claimed to be able to direct to his patients, he spoke of it as a universal "fluid" which pervades the universe. This energy, he claimed, could be drawn upon for healing the physical body. It was found in actual healing practice that if the magnetizer or healer believed this idea of the universal fluid to be true, and held this belief firmly in his mind, he did not tend to become depleted of energy when treating many patients one after the other. On the other hand, if he regarded the powers as being his own personal power, he quickly became depleted if he treated more than a certain limited number of patients at one session. Even when the belief in the universal fluid was firmly held, too long a session would produce temporary depletion, and the healer had to rest a while.

This recalls the words attributed to Jesus when he healed the woman with the issue of blood. She touched Him in the midst of the crowd which was pressing around Him, and the disciples were quite right, of course, when He said, "Who touched me?" to reply, "Thou seest the crowd, and sayest thou 'who touched me?' " I have seen a similar scene in the east when a wandering *sannyasi* or holy man came into a small village. The entire population clustered around him, trying to touch him.

The Bible story goes on to say that Jesus perceived that "virtue" had gone forth from Him. This word virtue was used by King James's translators of the authorized version of the Bible to stand for a Greek word that is the root from which such modern words as dynamo, dynamic, and dynamite were formed. It implies a strong, active energy, not what is usually thought of when we employ the term "virtue." The usual meaning attributed to the word is moral or ethical purity, more especially sexual purity.

The Power of Purity

This meaning really proceeds from the original meaning of the word, for it was widely held in ancient days that purity of life, and especially purity of sexual life, conferred power upon a person. It was even held that a virgin girl would not be attacked by a wild beast because of her virginity! This idea also led to the insistence, in medieval magic, upon the scryer or seer in the magical experiments being either a boy or girl below the age of puberty. Actually, for reasons of magnetic or etheric purity there is something in this latter idea. Also, men and women of pre-eminent moral and spiritual virtue have been known to pass unharmed through the haunts of vicious and predatory wild beasts, though they were closely watched and inspected by those beasts.

The cofounder of the Theosophical Society, Col. Henry Steele Olcott, did a great deal of magnetic healing during his stay in India and, in fact, so badly depleted himself that, upon the advice of an occult expert in such matters, he stopped this healing work and spent some time in recuperating his energies. The chief way in which he did this was, again upon the advice of his occult friend, to sit with his back against the trunk of a pine tree, and to allow the vital energies of the tree to recharge him.

Healing Techniques

Valentine Greatrakes in Ireland in the eighteenth century used magnetic healing technique by what is usually known as the "laying on of hands," and was, in fact, allocated a small pension from the British Government for his work. Father John of Kronstadt, a priest of the Orthodox Church, was not so fortunate. He so depleted himself that he ultimately died as a result of his healing work. There is a point to be noted here. Both Greatrakes and Father John regarded the power they used as being something that was not theirs, but for which they were a channel. Why then were they so depleted? The answer is that although there may be an inexhaustible supply, unless the channels through which that power is drawn into the human personality of the healer are sufficiently clear and open enough to allow all the power needed to flow in, there will be a gradual depletion of the healer's personal energies, and the only solution, at least for the short term outlook, is to stop doing healing work until the stock of energy has been renewed.

Magnetic healing is usually done by what is known as "passes" made with the hands over the body of the patient, or by the laying-on-of-hands or by the use of healing oils. Here we come to an interesting point in the study of these etheric energies. The etheric aura is not only a receiver of forces, but also a transmitter, and the energies that flow through it may be directed to other things besides human bodies. Animals may benefit from the forces directed upon them through the etheric aura, and so also may the vegetable kingdom. I have referred to the energy which Col. Olcott drew from the pine tree, but this is not one-way traffic. Just as we can draw etheric energy from the plants and trees, so can they draw from us when they, in their turn, need such help.

There have been many experiments made of this power of some human beings to affect for good or bad the lives of members of the vegetable kingdom, and it may well be that those who possess the traditional green thumbs are people with the power to transmit these energies to an ailing plant. That they do not consciously realize their possession of this power does not matter in the least; in fact it may often help, since their conscious mind is for the moment out of the way, and the subconscious has a chance to bring the etheric mechanism into action.

But not only can the etheric energies be transmitted to human beings, animals and plants. They can also be poured into and charge inanimate objects, such as stones, jewels, oils, and so on. These objects will then act as a kind of magnetic battery, pouring their charge of energy out as required.

When this charging or magnetizing is done by someone who understands the principles involved, the object so charged becomes not merely a battery that will discharge itself until its charge is exhausted, but will also be linked up with the universal energies, and so remain charged and potent for healing, or for any other purpose originally intended.

In the Roman Church the *Oleum Infirmorum*, the oil for the sick, is blessed by the bishop in his cathedral church on Maundy Thursday for use during the following year. However, healing oil may be prepared by anyone who understands the principle of magnetization.

A Cure with Oils

That the use of the healing oils may be effective was once demonstrated to me. It was in January of 1919, and I was at that time a patient in the Military Hospital in Glasgow, having been invalided from France in 1918. During my convalescence, I was invited to a healing demonstration being done by a small group of metaphysical healers. Their technique was to surround the patient with thoughts of healing, and to call down, from higher levels, the universal healing force. As it was known that I was a clairvoyant, they asked me to report on what I might see during the healing. This I did, and I was able to tell them that although the patient appeared to be surrounded by a deep blue cloud of energy, none of it was entering her body; it simply lay there like a pool of blue light enveloping her. She herself, on being questioned, said that she felt no different, and certainly no better.

It so happened that another occultist who was also present had some of the healing oils in his pocket, and it was suggested that he should use them on the patient. So unstoppering the small silver tube in which the healing oil was kept, he moistened his thumb with oil and just traced the sign of the Cross on the forehead of the patient.

At once things began to happen. To my sight it was as though a vortex was set up over the forehead of the subject, and the deep blue light seemed to pour down this in almost exactly the same way as the water in the bath or sink disappears when the plug is removed. Within a short time, all the energy had been absorbed into the patient's body. Not only did she say she felt much better, it was clearly evident that she was brighter and more alert, and appeared to be much improved.

It was explained that the magnetized oil had acted as a bridge between the finer energies which had been drawn down upon the patient and her own etheric body and aura. It was then possible for that energy to be drawn into the etheric aura and so made of some use.

A similar technique is used by some healers who magnetize handkerchiefs or linen pads and send them to their patients, and in this connection one thinks of the objects that were taken to the sick because the shadow of one of the Apostles had fallen on them. If we read "aura" for "shadow," we may see some significance in the Bible story.

The field of force we call the etheric aura is the field·in which many as yet unsuspected energies play. All the facts about the aura have yet to be discovered, and there are many fascinating lines of research for those so interested.

Etheric Interaction

The interactions between the etheric auras of people is another most interesting phenomenon. The spell-binder who can charm the birds down out of the trees, as the saying goes, has this ability because of a certain development in his etheric aura, and his intellectual or oratorical attainments have nothing to do with this power. There are others who act as destructive catalysts, and who, in any group, irrespective of what they may say or not say, will cause disruption and dissension. In the same way there are those who, because they are catalysts of the opposite order, will enable the members of a group to work together in an almost incredible fashion. Again, there are some who have the peculiar power to bring into action the latent abilities of others. This is noticeable in cases where a teacher who has a strong sense of vocation, apart from the purely material and professional aspect of his work, appears to be able to make such an intimate contact with the minds of his pupils as to evoke from them their own innate powers in a way that the ordinary teacher very often signally fails to do.

A curious variant of this power is that possessed by some who, by their presence alone, stimulate into activity the psychic abilities of those around them, though they themselves often display no such powers. Such people are useful members of what are known as "developing circles." It would seem that some part of their etheric aura has the property of inducing its own rate of vibration in the auras of others. Here we may also speculate as to whether the universal custom of the laying-on-of-hands for the transmission of priestly and other office may not have a basis in this property of the etheric. This would, of course, be strongly denied by those who vociferously insist that all men are equal and that no one has any power or ability that others have not got also. One might reply to this claim by suggesting that the ideal society would be one where each member brought his own particular and, perhaps, unique gift into the common pool for the benefit of all.

21

The Emotional-Mental Aura

IT is the custom of many writers on occult subjects to make a clearcut and definite division between the emotional and mental aspects of man's nature, and when considering the structure of the human entity to refer to the emotional or astral body and the mental body as two entirely separate parts of his being. This is, of course, quite correct if you are conducting what we might describe as a post-mortem on the complete man; that is, if you are studying him as an anatomist studies the human body. To the anatomist, there are certain well-defined systems of organs, nerves, etc., and these he sees, first of all as separate systems, such as the alimentary system, the vascular system, and so on, even though he always keeps at the back of his mind the overriding fact that all these systems in the living man are working together in a very wonderful way, and their individual activities are joined together for the common life of the individual.

Equally, of course, it is permissible to separate the emotional and mental aspects of man, and also the vehicles or bodies through which those aspects work, but when we come to consider the living individual, we find that in actual practice we cannot separate these two ways in which man expresses himself on the physical plane.

The Kama-Manasic Principle

This has been recognized in both the Eastern and Western occult traditions. In the East, the two activities of emotion and thought are grouped together under the term *Kama-Manas*, *Kama* meaning "desire" and *Manas* referring to "mind." Above this double aspect they also refer to the plane or level of pure thought by the term "the *Manasic* Plane."

In the Western tradition the same idea is found in the Qabalistic concept of what is termed the *Ruach* or "reasonable soul." They too say that above this realm there exists another region wherein that aspect of man which the Qabalists name the *Neschamah* or Higher Soul has its dwelling.

Although I follow the Western esoteric tradition, I am going to briefly attempt to separate these two elements of emotion and thought that go to make up the *Ruach* or *Kama-manasic* principle in man. I propose to deal with the emotional or astral aspect as being one in which force is predominant. There is a certain fundamental duality throughout the whole kingdoms of nature—a division into realms of force and realms of form. Each level is made up of these two aspects, but the proportions vary with the different levels of manifestation. Thus, the physical earth is a plane of form, but it is actually the appearance which is the result of interlocked forces. Its chief characteristic is that of inertia. It is a level of stability, and physical matter will not of itself change position unless acted upon by some outer force. The etheric levels of the physical are the force aspect, and matter as we see it is the form aspect of this physical level.

On the emotional or astral level, the positions are reversed. The substance of the astral light is characterized by extreme mobility; it is fluid and has the protean ability to take a thousand evanescent shapes as different influences affect it. In itself it can best be thought of as a realm of living light; light which can in an instant be built up into a temporary form.

Symbols

There are two main building or form-producing causes at work in the astral realms. One is the influence that is always at work molding the tenuous astral substance in obedience to its own basic laws. These forms which are, so to speak, native to the astral light, cannot be perceived by the average human clairvoyant, for they are so far from all human experience that there is nothing in the clairvoyant's mind by which such forms can be comprehended. The only way in which these native forms can be brought into the waking consciousness is by the deliberate use of symbols, and it is for this reason that many seers have found it necessary to resort to the use of symbolism to transmit even a small part of the astral perception to the conscious mind. But such use of symbols demands considerable training in their use and understanding so those who have not undergone a definite training along those lines do not, as a general rule perceive the native forms in the astral light, except where certain well-established symbols have been constructed by generations of men. Then, under earthly veils, these things are perceived.

Form from Mental Activity

The other form building process on the level of the astral light is that of thought, both conscious and subconscious. The mental levels are form levels, as opposed to the force levels of the astral light, and it is the form produced by mental activity that is thrown into the astral realms and immediately becomes charged with the force of that level. So in the astral light, there are to be found multitudinous images built up by the action of thought from the plastic fluid substance of that level.

Some of these forms and images are as transient as the ripple produced by the passing breeze playing upon the still surface of a lake, but others are far more lasting, and provide the semi-permanent scenery of the astral world. Of such are the "heavens" and "hells" and "grey worlds" so commonly described in spiritualist literature, and to those who live in them they do constitute a scenery and background that reflects, to a greater or lesser degree, the scenery and conditions of the earth itself.

The thoughts produce these "mansions," these temporary resting-places of the human spirit in the astral world, are the results of conscious and subconscious thinking on the part of humanity both incarnate and discarnate, as well as the mental activity of other non-human life which shares this level with man and closely influences him, though he may not be aware of it.

I cannot go into greater detail concerning these astral levels in the limited scope of this book, but I have mentioned this power of the mind to build forms. Our thinking builds forms in our astro-mental aura, even as the collective thinking of the whole of humanity builds up the forms in the astral light, or, to give it its modern name, the collective unconscious.

So, to the clairvoyant eye, the aura appears as a luminous colored atmosphere surrounding everyone. The extent of this second aura will vary according to the emotional and mental development of the person observed, as will also its coloring. This coloring will range from dark and muddy-looking shades of brown and grey, through lurid reds and dirty-looking blues, to the finer shades of these colors and to fine luminous yellow, blue and violet shades. There may also appear gleams of pure golden light, but these are usually rare.

In this shining atmosphere around each person may also be noticed forms of various kinds, and it is here that mistakes may often arise when a description of the aura is being given. There are often human figures to be seen in the aura, but these need not have anything to do with the actual life, being merely thought-forms that have been built up by casual contacts with people who, for one reason or another, have left a strong imprint on the mind of the person whose aura is being observed.

Subconscious Memories

There are other finer and more subtle forms which are often only outcropping memories from the subconscious, and it sometimes happens that something is described by the seer and is immediately recognized by the person concerned. Very often he will say, "It couldn't be telepathy, for I wasn't thinking about that thing at all." However, this is what it could probably be in truth, since these thought forms can act as the end of a long line of associated memories that are evoked, as it were, from the depths of the subconscious. Of course, this does not cover all such forms, but it certainly seems to account for a good deal of so-called evidence.

Occasionally such forms seen and described by the clairvoyant turn out to be nothing more than vivid images built up in the mind of a person through reading a book which portrays such characters. Thus one lady was told by a clairvoyant, "I see a strange figure with you. Have you anything to do with the sea? For I see the figure of a man who would be a seaman of some kind, and who possibly fought in some sea battle, for I see he has only one leg. I see around him what seems to be tropical vegetation and I get a strong feeling of violence and bloodshed." The person to whom this description was given smiled and said "Yes, I recognize the figure—you see I have just been reading Robert Louis Stevenson's book *Treasure Island*"!

It is difficult for even the experienced seer to always detect the difference between these thought forms and other forms which may come into the aura from other sources. Only practice over a long period will enable him to do this, and even then he may often be mistaken.

The second part of the emotional-mental aura is the

luminous appearance that spreads around the person. In some it may only extend about a couple of feet, but with others its range is far more extensive. It remains now to deal with this luminous atmosphere from a consideration of the colors to be found in it.

Spirit and Matter Not Opposed

Here I must say that often the mistake is made of equating the finer pastel shades of color with the spiritual nature, while the more vivid and denser shades are held to be indications of the earthly side of the self. This is a mistaken view. It is true to a certain point, but it often gives a totally false idea of the character of the person. First of all, such a view accepts the idea of material and spiritual as being two sharply divided opposites like the East and West in Kipling's poem, "Never the twain shall meet." This was the error of the Gnostics, or some of them, in the early Christian Church, and in one form or another it has persisted through the centuries. The truer view, in the opinion of many of us, is that both spirit and matter are the expressions of a supreme reality; they are, as it were, the two poles of the cosmic battery, and the web of the universe is spun between them. In that field of energies all life and consciousness lives and moves and has its being. There are those institutions wherein this is symbolized by the two Pillars of Solomon's Temple; between these lies the tessellated pavement of black and white squares, and our human pilgrimage means that we are never wholly treading upon a black square or entirely upon a white one.

This is reflected in our individual private universe, and reveals itself in the aura. It is an over-simplification to divide humanity into "goodies" and "baddies," in the tradition of Wild West films. We are a mixed bag, and there are both good and evil aspects in each one of us. There used to be a doggerel rhyme which stated, "There's so much good in the worst of us, and so much bad in the best of us," and this is true. There are aspects of our nature that are of the higher part, and there are other aspects that are of the lower side of ourselves, and there is a large part of our emotional-mental make-up that is the reflection of a mixture of both of these aspects. According to the general activity of these factors we build up what we may term the permanent background of the aura. It is this general coloring that usually shows us as we are, and this is fairly stable, changing slowly or otherwise as we progress through life.

However, there are times when the more elemental parts of our nature suddenly emerge into activity, and their activity is shown by the fiery and turgid shades of color that show themselves in the aura. In the same way, there are times when the ethical and spiritual aspects of ourselves also come into activity, and such activity is shown by the finer shades of color. But both of these conditions may only be, most probably will be, of short duration and their appearance does not give a clue as to the real character of the person in whose aura they are seen.

Significance of Pastel Shades

Often an aura showing all the color in fine pastel shades may well indicate a personality without any positive will or emotional drive, and such people, although regarded by their friends as most spiritual, are only to be so thought of in a negative way. I think it is Milton who somewhere says, "I would not praise a cloistered virtue which has never been subjected to temptation." In the same way, the aura very often indicates that, far from its possessor being highly evolved he is in fact quite unevolved in some important ways, and it may also indicate the near total repression of part of the nature.

Because of this, it is difficult to correctly assess the true level of character of anyone by simply reading his aura, unless one has built up by practice the ability to watch the permanent aura when the nature is being subjected to stress. It is under these conditions that the true character of a person can be discerned. I have told the following story before in another book of mine, but it will bear repetition, as it illustrates a mistake so many make in supposing that the suppression of all physical signs of any particular emotion indicates that one has gained control over it.

In a certain occult training college (for such establishments really do exist) the principal had a technique of his own. Each of the students had a small garden for which he or she were directly responsible. All these gardens were visible from the dining room and it sometimes happened that while at dinner, a student would look through the window and see his or her little garden being ruined by the activities of one of several animals kept at the place. They were supposed to look at this wanton destruction without any display of emotion, even though it meant that many hours of work had passed in vain. (The presence of the animal in the garden concerned had been carefully engineered by the principal himself.)

The one who told me of this, who was herself one of these students, said that she found herself perfectly able to watch her gardening efforts being brought to naught because, as she put it, she had been blessed with a good "poker face"! Under her calm and placid appearance, however, she was seething with indignation and busy working out various punishments that might fit the crime.

It is far better to release such emotions than to repress them violently into the depths of the mind, and, of course, it is better still to learn to control the *inner* reactions rather than the physical expressions thereof. Such repressions result in a churning up of the mind that is reflected in the aura.

Projection of Thought Forms

Incidentally, in the emotional-mental aura there are to be found many forms that have been built up in the mind, but most of these are vague and indistinct. The emotional-mental aura, like the etheric aura, has an outer limit which seems to act as a kind of protective skin, though the radiations of the aura pass through it for considerable distances. It is through these radiations that what we call telepathy takes place, but most of the thought forms built up in the aura never have the energy needed to project them beyond the outer limit of their creator's aura. Like sparks from the blacksmith's anvil, when the white-hot iron is struck by the hammer, such thought sparks fly upwards, but are almost immediately quenched and never go beyond the brief area around them. Two things are necessary for the successful projection of such thought forms beyond the aura, and these two things are clearness of form and strength of charge. The successful building up of forms in the mind is something that cannot usually be acquired in a short time; it takes a period of steady training, unless the one who is building the forms has some innate ability in this direction. This does sometimes happen, and then, one of the conditions being fulfilled, it remains to see how the form can be charged with the energy that will enable it to be projected to a distance.

This is done by a process of brooding over the thought, and by brooding over I mean a steady *emotional* concentration upon it. It is for this reason that so many experiments in thought transference fail. The form of the thought may have been visualized and built up clearly, but since no emotional force is connected with it, there is no power to project it upon its way. This is not always the case, for there is some evidence to suggest that, sometimes, the receiver's mind reaches out toward the mind of the sender, and reads therein the picture or symbol that he is wishing to transmit.

Dissociated Complexes

The thought forms that accumulate within the aura because of suppression and inhibition have a strong influence upon the character of the individual, and even more so are those emotionally charged groups of thoughts which are known to the psychologists as "dissociated complexes." These dissociated complexes have been thrust out from the normal circulation of the mind, and have become semi-independent. Because of the strong emotional charge within them, they come into conflict with the normal processes of the mind, and the resulting battle means that most of the available energy of the personality is locked up and cannot be used. So arise the various troubles that are the symptoms of this underlying fight and it is vitally important in every way that some contact with this semi-independent complex which is throttling the inflow of energy should be gained. Modern psychologists have a useful method of doing this—the so-called word association test. Certain words are said to the patient, and he is asked to give the first word that comes into his mind as soon as he has heard the test word. The time before he is able to produce such a word that arises from the depths within him varies widely. With some of the association words he will produce his own reaction-word almost immediately, but with others there is often a complete inability to produce any reaction, or a reaction word will only come up in his mind after quite a long time. The actual reaction times are usually taken by means of a stopwatch.

This method has proved helpful, though it has also been found that a certain self-protective device in the subconscious has produced a substitute reaction word, in order to stop any further probing. Sometimes, such substitute words may be as revealing as those for which they stand, but on the other hand, they may be wildly misleading.

The reaction word is used as the beginning of a chain of what is known as free association, as the patient is asked to let his mind go free and allow the reaction word to start any trains of thought it will. By the use of several of the test words, several such trains of free association may be started, and they will often be found to be converging toward some central idea. Somewhere in this region lies the contact with the semi-independent thought complex and if it is successfully contacted, the repressed thoughts and memories surge into consciousness, together with the powerful charge of energy they have held, and, after a period of readjustment, the patient's mind is restored to normal working.

However, if by the use of psychic vision the dissociated complex can be seen in the emotional-mental aura of the patient, it is then possible to *gently* disclose it to the patient, thus avoiding the distressing uprush of emotional energy which so often happens when the complex is contacted. The reeducation whereby the *cause* of the dissociation can be removed from the personality can then proceed much more rapidly than otherwise. Also, where the patient's subconscious mind has shown itself capable of fabricating imaginary memories and situations of the past, it is possible to get behind the defenses, as it were, and see directly into the creative area of the mind, and so cease to be deceived by the fantasies the sick mind may build up.

Some years ago I knew a psychic who discovered that she possessed this ability to see the thought forms within the aura of patients undergoing psychoanalytical treatment, and as she said, she found herself able to proceed directly to the reeducation of the mind without going through the lengthy and often distressing procedure involved in the usual word tests. As she was at the time a worker with a quite orthodox (in the medical sense) clinic in London, and was also one of the first *lay* psychoanalysts in this country, her testimony may be of value.

Meanings of the Colors

I have refrained from giving any meanings to the colors that may be seen in the aura. There are several books that give the conventional meanings, but in my own experience I have found that almost every person who develops psychic vision tends to have his own individual meaning which he attaches to the colors he sees, and for him these meanings are correct. Another psychic may well have a different set of meanings, and for him these may also be correct. The trouble arises when an attempt is made to enforce a system true for all. It can be done, and in certain occult schools it *is* done, but it takes a lot of hard work, and as long as the clairvoyant finds that *his* interpretations of the colors he sees are correct, he may well leave his brother psychic to the use of *his* system.

Purity of the Colors

One point that all clairvoyants are agreed on is the purity of the colors seen, and by this I do not mean the pale pastel shades, which are usually indicative of repressed or depleted vitality. A color can be strong as well as clear; what is necessary is that it shall not be contaminated by any mixture from another color. The images and thoughts derived from the experiences of earth are all to some extent so contaminated, although the degree may vary, and in the same way the images and thoughts that are influenced by the realms of the upper mind and spirit are usually irradiated by a starry luminosity which is quite unlike anything to be found in this material level. So the way in which the colors are shaded by earthly hues, or illumined by the starry radiance of the realms of true mind and spirit will give to the clairvoyant some indication of the general character of the person observed but it is only when the aura is observed during a time when its owner is under the test. of trial and temptation that the *true* character can be gauged.

The truly spiritual aura appears as a pervading radiance that informs both the etheric and emotional-mental auras, and streams beyond them, and in one who is advanced on the spiritual path it is one of the most wonderful sights ever seen by the seer. At the same time, it should be observed that any clairvoyant will as a general rule see only that to which he himself can respond, and consequently the higher aspects of what a recent writer has called "The Robe of Many Colors" are far beyond the reach of the average clairvoyant.

There are many fascinating things concerning this astro-mental aura and the forms and forces to be seen therein which I have been unable to touch upon within the compass of this book, but hope that sufficient has been given to interest and help those who may now or in the future try to work along these lines of study and research.

22

Developing Auric Sight

THERE are several ways in which auric sight may be
developed. One of these, as I have indicated in another section is to use what are known as the "Kilner
Screens," named after their inventor, Dr. Kilner. These
consist of glass cells containing a solution of certain dyes,
usually dycyanine and pinacol, both coal-tar derivatives.
By looking through the colored liquid in the cells at a
source of light for a period, the mechanism of the eyes is
slightly changed, and it begins to respond to the etheric
emanations given off from the body. Full details of the
procedure to be adopted are given by the manufacturers
of these "auric goggles."

Reading the Aura by Touch

However, it may not be possible for you to obtain such
goggles, and you are then forced to use one of the other
methods. Curiously enough, one method of reading the
aura is by touch! This calls for great care, as it is somewhat difficult, especially in the early stages, to get a clear
idea of what you are really getting. The way of using the
sense of touch for auric perception is as follows.

First you enlist the services of a sympathetic friend.
He either sits in a straight-backed chair, or else lies on a

couch. Then you pass your hand slowly downwards over his body, keeping it about two to three inches away from the actual surface of the body. This is most important; *never actually touch the physical body of your subject.* It is not necessary and will indeed, prevent you doing any sensing of his aura. I have italicized this because I have known this instruction to be ignored by some whose motives were somewhat mixed and had very little to do with auric research.

Now, as you slowly pass your hand downward over the subject, focus your attention upon the tips of your fingers, and try to sense any difference in the sensations you have in them as you move your hand away for about eight or nine inches, or bring it to about a couple of inches from the body. At first, and for a good many attempts, you may perceive nothing, but this is often because you have never had to concentrate upon your fingertips in this way, and other sensations will overpower the fine impressions that you may be receiving. There will come a time, however, when you will perceive that "something" that seems warm or cold or vibrant appears to be present some distance from the surface of the physical body of your subject. When you have experienced this, you can go to work to find out just how far from the subject's body this "something" extends, and you will then be able to experiment to see what shape the field of force takes. It is good training technique to spend some time before the experiments in preparing a number of rough drawings of the human body, front, back and side views. It is a good idea to have these Xeroxed, so that they are ready whenever you want to do an auric reading. The drawings can be used in marking down the variations you may find to exist in the aura. This first aura you will be observing is, of course, the etheric aura. Later you will wish to try to perceive the astro-mental aura which extends a good deal farther out from the body, and you will then move your hands at a greater distance, say a foot or so from the physical body of your subject.

Now it may well happen, though not in all cases, that as you begin to perceive or sense the aura, pictures will build up in your mind, and these may take the form of a silvery replica of the subject's body, which will show the same variations you are sensing in the aura. You will be seeing the aura subjectively, and this is a quite common form of development. At the same time, there are many who never "see" anything at all, but who do get a clear perception of the aura, its variations and other peculiarities. So do not be discouraged if you do not develop the subjective visual perception; the nonvisual intuitive perception may be far more accurate once you have learned to trust it. It has been described as "seeing a black cat at midnight at the bottom of a coal mine," and although this may sound ridiculous, I can assure you from my own personal experience of this type of vision, that you really do see the black cat, and what is more, you learn more about him than you might have done if you had actually perceived him visually.

Intuitive Perception of Thought Forms

The other images that may form in your mind as visual pictures, or be perceived intuitively, are usually the thought forms that are in the aura, and these are of two main varieties. One group is made up of those thought forms that are the results of the mental and emotional activity of the person himself, and the other group is composed of those forms built up by other people. There are several reasons why these latter forms should be found in the aura. Sometimes they have been projected toward the person by others who have been thinking clearly and intensely about him, and have put a good deal of emotion into the process. This gives the forms their motive power and they are projected beyond their auric boundary and arrive with sufficient force to enable them to lodge in the aura of the one to whom they have been directed. This projection may be entirely unconsciously initiated; the one who is thinking so intensely of another person may not dream that he is possibly sending out such a form. There are others, however, who have a good working knowledge of this process, and are well aware of what they are doing. Those who have been wisely instructed do not do this kind of psychic trespass, for the penetration of the aura of another person in this way is the "breaking of a superficies"—the "removing of his neighbor's landmarks," and in both the Craft and in the Bible such a proceeding is regarded as wrong, and as meriting punishment.

Where, however, the surface of the aura is loose and not strongly built up, it will easily take in any thought forms that may strike on it, and such people go around with an aura which, from the clairvoyant point of view, is decidedly septic!

Because of this poorly built auric skin, it is sufficient for such people to pick up, like human fly-papers, any forms that may be about, and such forms may not always be of an exalted kind. Such people also leak vitality, and develop what is known as the orbicular wound.

As you begin to develop your ability to perceive these things, you will also find that you become aware of the measures that should be taken if the person concerned is to be brought back to full physical and emotional-mental stability. I have included this last remark because it often assists in the successful development of auric vision if you have a definite feeling that by the use of such vision you may be of help to others. Man is what has been described as a gregarious animal, which simply means that it is natural for us to group together, and in the conditions which this causes, most people find that to be able to help others in some way or other gives them an increased pleasure in living. Of course, this basic urge in man is often smothered beneath a code of selfishness and egotism, but every now and then it shows itself, often in the most unlikely people. When this desire to help does emerge its satisfaction brings to most of us a feeling that in some way we have moved beyond ourselves, and in a mysterious fashion enlarged ourselves. Although we may deviate considerably from the ideal of selfless service, as we develop, our general inclination will be to make use of these faculties in the service of others as well as ourselves.

Auric Sight by Direct Vision

There is yet another way in which this faculty of auric sight may be developed, and that is by direct vision. At the same time, there is a trap into which you may easily fall, which consists of staring in such a fixed way at the person that the mechanism of your eyes becomes fatigued and shifts the focus and consequently the position of the image that is falling upon the retina, the screen of the eye. The resulting flash of color, usually yellow or golden, which appears around the person being observed is often mistaken for the aura, whereas it is simply the result of optical fatigue.

So in attempting this particular way of seeing the aura, you must not stare fixedly at the person. The best results are obtained when the one whom you are observing stands against a dark background, preferably in a north light. As you are trying to see a fine emanation that may at first, since the etheric aura is the most easily perceived at the beginning of development, be only some two inches away from the surface of the body, it is best if the subject of your vision wears close-fitting clothes. Indeed, many people find that they get the best results when the clothing worn consists simply of vest and trousers, or swimming trunks. Here, of course, you must use your common sense. A married man who insisted upon observing a bikini-clad damsel could be asking for trouble, unless she was his wife. If I seem (as some of my previous remarks would suggest) somewhat prudish in my attitude toward this question of near-nudity, it is because I have had a fairly lengthy experience of these matters over a period of fifty years, and in any case it is inadvisable to introduce unnecessary distractions in an exercise that is difficult enough by itself!

The subject now standing against the dark background, the observer sits and gazes quietly and without any strain at him, at the same time throwing the eyes slightly out of focus. This is done by actually focusing them about six to nine inches beyond the subject. This will mean that his actual form will be only vaguely discernible, although its general outlines will be sufficiently clear. This refocusing of the eye is a little trick that may take some time for you to master, but by quietly and repeatedly attempting it, you will eventually gain proficiency. I have emphasized "quietly," for there must be no strain, no undue physical effort. The faculty you are attempting to develop is already within your subconscious mind, and, indeed, the better word would be unfoldment, rather than development. Any conscious effort will simply get in the way of the emergence of the faculty.

It is helpful if, before you start the session, you sit down quietly, relax as well as you can, and then, again without any strain, quietly tell yourself, and of course your subconscious self, that you are now going to allow the faculty of super-normal vision to unfold itself. You can use whatever form of words you like, as long as they convey the idea and are positive in their meaning. For instance, you would not tell yourself that you are going to "try" to unfold your vision. This is not positive enough. You are now going to allow the faculty to unfold. How far it does actually unfold itself in any one session is something you will not be able to gauge, but you may rest assured that every time you so affirm your intention to allow it to take place, some unfoldment will actually occur.

When you have mastered the technique of refocusing the eyes, and the parallel technique of the positive intention, you may begin to look for anything you may perceive around the subject. Usually it will take the form of a misty grey luminosity which seems to extend around the subject's body, and at this stage check to make sure that you have not inadvertently begun to use a fixed stare. If you find that this is not the case, and that you are really seeing this luminous haze around the subject, you can then go on to note any peculiarities that may affect the aura. For instance, it may have a pronounced bulge over one particular part of the body, or it may have sunk back almost to the surface of the body. Using the sketches of the human figure in outline you should note this down, after the observation is finished. If you try to see and mark at the same time, you will find that the activity so caused will tend to break your vision. Of course you could have a tape recorder running, and by having the various parts of your outline diagram numbered, it would be possible for you to quietly observe, "There's a big bulge over section 7" or wherever it may be seen.

What usually happens in the first session in which you actually do see anything is that your excitement tends to arouse you from the particular mental state you have reached, and the vision is lost for that time at least. With practice, however, you learn not to allow any unwanted emotion to blur the surface of the mental mirror reflecting the impressions that are coming in by way of the subconscious.

The subject should change position and stand sideways to you for a time. Or put his hand upon his hip and so allow you to look for the somewhat denser aura that will be in the space between his arms and his body.

The Fingers Experiment

To give the subject a rest, you can conduct a few experiments for yourself by holding your two hands with the fingers almost touching each other and then slowly moving them apart, using the same dark background. You will see, if the faculty is beginning to work, what appear to be bands of greyish light that run from the fingers of one hand to those of the other. This, too, could be an optical illusion, and this you may test by lowering one hand six or nine inches below the other. You will then see how these rays still connect the fingers, but are now running in a diagonal direction between them. At a later date you can try to project the grey light from any one selected finger, and see what happens. Also you can see whether these rays will flow between your hand and that of your friend, the subject. Try the two right hands and then the two left hands, and then the left and right hands of you both and see what difference it makes. There are interesting polarity effects that you may notice, and these will suggest other experiments you may carry out.

After you have begun to perceive the aura, and as an interesting variant on observing the auras of people, you may try, using the same general technique of lighting, etc., to observe the auras of plants and, when outside conditions permit, the auras of trees. At a later date, you should extend your observations to cover the radiations given off by minerals of various kinds. All such experiments can be of the greatest interest, and if careful records are kept, more especially when the faculty is becoming fairly well established, you may possibly discover aspects of the aura that have not hitherto been described. For this is a large field of research, and those who use the power of auric vision are usually operating in one sector only, depending upon whether they are working with a religious group, a research group, a magical group, or simply as solitary students of the subject.

Although I have dealt with clairvoyance and psychometry in other sections, it is well to realize that these are but the separate manifestations of the one faculty of psychic perception. The clairvoyant and psychometric powers are but specialized expressions of this one psychic sense, and in actual practice you will often find that one aspect shades off into one of the others. As a general rule this does not matter greatly, unless you are working exclusively along one line of work.

Patience Is Essential

Finally, I would like to briefly mention the time factor. No one can tell you how long it may be before you develop the faculty, for this depends on many considerations. A friend of mine sitting for this development took seven years before he had any results whatsoever. This was an extreme case, but you must be prepared to exercise quite a lot of patience, unless you are one of those in whom the faculty is near the surface of consciousness. Always remember, however, that true development should result in a well-balanced character. It is far better to have five senses and sanity than to have acquired a sixth sense that causes you to be unbalanced and unreliable in your personal and social life. So it is as well, if you decide to develop this, or any other psychic faculty, to carefully consider your present personality, and try to assess your readiness for such psychic development. As we are usually the worst possible judges of our own personalities, it is helpful to try to get the opinions of those with whom we come into fairly close contact, and this does not mean that you should choose as your critics only those with whom you are on friendly terms. A great deal can be learned from someone who dislikes you, and who is not afraid to tell you so to your face. It could be, of course, that in some judgments he is wrong, as he may not be in a position to know all the things in your life that make you to be as you appear. Allowing for this, it may still be true that criticism is of more value to you than the kindly evaluation of your friends! In any case, it is always a good mental and moral discipline to be strong enough to consider such adverse criticism without reacting to it in an emotional and ill-balanced way.

Remember that what you are inviting criticism on is the unfinished temple of your personality. Any defect that you are now building into it may well imperil the whole structure when, at a later date, it is subjected to greater strain. It is, therefore, true wisdom to consider the critic who points to defects and deficiencies, and then take a long cool look at these alleged defects and deficiencies. It may well be that some of them have been overstressed, but it may also be true that in some measure they are to be regarded as things that are to be seen in your personality, and they should be attended to before you go on to attempt the building of a new aspect of your personal temple.

The Safeguard of Humility

There is yet another way in which you may err. in these matters. When you have at last developed the faculty, it is easy to form an exaggerated idea of your own importance, and to feel that you ought to be regarded as "Sir Oracle." This is a common temptation, and one that is almost certain to be ministered to by unwise friends who will attempt to put you upon a pedestal from which you may deliver the oracles of the gods. I have mentioned this in previous sections because it is one of the most common troubles in the whole field of psychic development, and it can lead to untold trouble.

Sooner or later, due to the natural fluctuations of the psychic perceptions, the time comes when you are no longer able to deliver the goods, and if you are honest and admit that for the time being you are not able to fulfill the demands made on you, you will probably be somewhat surprised to find with what indecent rapidity you are removed from the seat of the oracle, and your followers go hunting for another who, in his turn, they may elevate to that position!

It is best, then, at all times, to be modest in your claims. Those who are really interested and sincere will not hold it against you that at certain times you cannot give what is wanted, nor will they be inclined to cavil because you do not make any high-sounding claims for yourself and your gift.

It is for this reason, among others, that the occult

schools usually impress upon their pupils that they must not use the psychic faculties they develop for monetary end. The commercial use of the psychic faculties brings many temptations, chief among which is the tendency to indulge in fraud when the faculty is having one of its off days. There are those who claim that the positive seer never has off days, and tend to regard in a supercilious fashion those who admit to such lapses.

However, in many years of practical experience in this field, I have come to the conclusion that the distinction cannot be upheld. The positive seer may be less prone to such things than his negative brother, but I have no doubt that at times, even for him, "the heavens are as brass" and he gets little or nothing through his psychic faculties.

If you are free from the necessity of having to demonstrate the psychic faculty for payment, then you are free from many of the troubles that may otherwise come to you. What is more, you will be able to express your own opinion in these fields without the fear of annoying those upon whose goodwill your finances depend.

The development of the psychic faculties has hitherto been mainly under the aegis of religious organizations, and they have been pressed into service to prove this or that tenet of the particular organization. This is not always helpful, for religion is one of the aspects of life where the feelings are closely concerned, and where they can easily override the facts. The psychic realm has its own laws, and not all of what is perceived by psychic perception will agree with the dogmatic statements of religious organizations. Whether the psychic is wrong in his observations, which is always possible, or whether the dogma of the organization needs expansion or restatement, or whether the discrepancy springs from both causes, the net result may well be quite a lot of trouble for the psychic whose findings do not agree with the religious organization concerned. For this reason, it is my own personal opinion that these things should be studied in a neutral manner, and should not be resorted to in order to support the claims of any one religious sect.

However, to essay this development under the aegis

of a religious organization does bring in the question of moral issues, and it is here that religion can enable the psychic to direct his research into such channels that he may be the better able to serve God and his fellow man.

Books of Related Interest

Pendulum Power
A Mystery You Can See, A Power You Can Feel
by Greg Nielsen and Joseph Polansky

Techniques of High Magic
A Handbook of Divination, Alchemy, and the Evocation of Spirits
by Francis King and Stephen Skinner

Energy Vampires
A Practical Guide for Psychic Self-protection
by Dorothy Harbour

Entity Possession
Freeing the Energy Body of Negative Influences
by Samuel Sagan, M.D.

Chakras
Energy Centers of Transformation
by Harish Johari

How to Read Signs and Omens in Everyday Life
by Sarvananda Bluestone, Ph.D.

Psychonavigation
Techniques for Travel Beyond Time
by John Perkins

The World Is As You Dream It
Shamanic Teachings from the Amazon and Andes
by John Perkins

Inner Traditions • Bear & Company
P.O. Box 388
Rochester, VT 05767
1-800-246-8648
www.InnerTraditions.com
Or contact your local bookseller